The growth of big business
in the United States and
western Europe, 1850–1939

New Studies in Economic and Social History

Edited for the Economic History Society by
Michael Sanderson
University of East Anglia, Norwich

This series, specially commissioned by the Economic History Society, provides a guide to the current interpretations of the key themes of economic and social history in which advances have recently been made or in which there has been significant debate.

In recent times economic and social history has been one of the most flourishing areas of historical study. This has mirrored the increasing relevance of the economic and social sciences both in a student's choice of career and in forming a society at large more aware of the importance of these issues in their everyday lives. Moreover specialist interests in business, agricultural and welfare history, for example, have themselves burgeoned and there has been an increased interest in the economic development of the wider world. Stimulating as these scholarly developments have been for the specialist, the rapid advance of the subject and the quantity of new publications make it difficult for the reader to gain an overview of particular topics, let alone the whole field.

New Studies in Economic and Social History is intended for students and their teachers. It is designed to introduce them to fresh topics and to enable them to keep abreast of recent writing and debates. All the books in the series are written by a recognised authority in the subject, and the arguments and issues are set out in a critical but unpartisan fashion. The aim of the series is to survey the current state of scholarship, rather than to provide a set of prepackaged conclusions.

The series has been edited since its inception in 1968 by Professors M. W. Flinn, T. C. Smout and L. A. Clarkson, and is currently edited by Dr Michael Sanderson. From 1968 it was published by Macmillan as *Studies in Economic History*, and after 1974 as *Studies in Economic and Social History*. From 1995 *New Studies in Economic and Social History* is being published on behalf of the Economic History Society by Cambridge University Press. This new series includes some of the titles previously published by Macmillan as well as new titles, and reflects the ongoing development throughout the world of this rich seam of history.

For a full list of titles in print, please see the end of the book.

The growth of big business in the United States and western Europe, 1850–1939

Prepared for the Economic History Society by

Christopher J. Schmitz
University of St Andrews

Published by the Press Syndicate of the University of Cambridge
The Pitt Building, Trumpington Street, Cambridge CB2 1RP
40 West 20th Street, New York, NY 10011-4211, USA
10 Stamford Road, Oakleigh, Melbourne 3166, Australia

*The growth of big business in the United States and Western Europe,
1850–1939* first published by The Macmillan Press Limited 1993
First Cambridge University Press edition 1995

Printed in Great Britain at the University Press, Cambridge

A catalogue record for this book is available from the British Library

Library of Congress cataloguing in publication data applied for

ISBN 0 521 55282 6 hardback
ISBN 0 521 55771 2 paperback

CE

Contents

Figures

Tables

Acknowledgements

I should like to thank Clive Lee, Peter Payne, Richard Saville and Christopher Smout, for extremely helpful comments on earlier versions of the manuscript, as well as Leslie Clarkson for his help as series editor at the time that this study was first written. I should, in addition, like to extend my thanks to Leslie Hannah, for a number of suggestions which have been incorporated into this revised edition of the book. My ideas have also been strongly influenced by succeeding generations of students in my 'Big Business' class at St Andrews, who acted as critical guinea-pigs with earlier drafts of the text. Apologies are offered where I have failed to heed their collective advice, and responsibility is accepted for any imperfections that inevitably remain in such a concise account.

Note

In order to facilitate comparisons between countries, monetary data have been converted, where possible, to United States dollars at contemporary exchange rates. References in the text to billions represent thousands of millions.

1
Introduction

Few things epitomise economic change in the twentieth century world more than the rise and spread of giant business corporations. By the 1980s, organisations like General Motors, Royal Dutch-Shell and Siemens had grown to vast proportions, each employing hundreds of thousands of people around the globe and selling products valued in tens of billions of dollars a year. Yet, little more than a century earlier such leviathans of capitalism scarcely existed. During the 1850s and 1860s, modern forms of large-scale business enterprise had only emerged in a few limited areas, such as the railway industry. The next half century witnessed a business revolution, in which an ever-widening range of manufacturing, mining and service companies in the industrial economies adopted structural forms pioneered by the railways. By the 1930s the process was by no means complete, but the essential features of global big business had already taken shape.[1] An increasing part of economic transactions in the United States and western Europe was by then organised within integrated, multi-plant firms, engaged in a wide variety of activities, and commonly owning subsidiaries in a number of different countries. These enterprises were not just characterised by their scale of operations and huge work-forces. Unlike their counterparts of a century earlier, they were less frequently managed by their owners, but by a new class of salaried executives, organised in complex hierarchies of middle and upper management. Ownership in such firms was no longer commonly represented by intimate groups of entrepreneurs or family members, but by seemingly anonymous bodies of thousands of individual shareholders as well as large-scale institutional investors.

A pronounced example of this trend was the United States Steel Corporation, which in 1929 was one of the world's largest industrial companies, with gross assets of $2.3 billion, a quarter of a million employees and over 182,000 stockholders. The largest single stockholding represented less than 0.75 per cent of issued capital, while the entire board of directors only held 1.4 per cent (Berle and Means, 1932; *87, 109*). In contrast, a century earlier, one of the largest industrial enterprises in Britain (and the world), the Cyfartha iron works in South Wales, had a capitalisation equivalent to around $2 million. It employed approximately 5000 men in 1830 and was closely owned and personally directed by a succession of members of the Crawshay family (Pollard, 1965; *22, 77-8*).

There are two key problems in understanding the historical evolution of large-scale business organisations: how and why they developed in the first place, and what factors have placed an upper limit on their growth. These two lines of inquiry in turn beg a series of subsidiary questions. Why did the growth of big business occur at different speeds and take on distinctive forms in different societies? Why has big business developed to a greater extent in some industries rather than others? If there have been upper limits to the growth of firms, have these remained static over time or, as seems more likely, have these limits changed? In addition, there is the separate, but equally important, question of the welfare implications of the rise of big business.

The subject is complex and made more difficult by the different directions from which academic study has proceeded to examine it. For far too long, economic and business historians tended to concern themselves with describing the growth of individual firms or industries, without making much attempt to relate their findings to economic or managerial theory (Coleman, 1987; *151–2*). Meanwhile economists, sociologists and management scientists were generating an impressive but woefully fragmented collection of theories relevant to the growth of big business. As a recent survey suggests, 'since ideas on the economics of the firm have developed in a number of different directions, it is difficult to make general statements about their common attributes' (Clarke and McGuinness, 1987; *1*). It is also difficult to discuss big business in a value-free way. Few topics have aroused antagonism across such a broad political spectrum: from interwar fascists, who associated large corporations with an ill-defined 'conspiracy' of international finance; through the American liberal antitrust tradition; to Marxists, who regard big business as a devious regeneration of an ailing capitalist system.

Given these problems, one of the most influential research contributions in this area during the past quarter-century has been the work of the American historian Alfred D. Chandler. His books *Strategy and Structure* (1962), *The Visible Hand* (1977) and *Scale and Scope* (1990) have provided a series of invaluable generalisations about the rise of the modern large-scale business corporation in America and Europe. What can usefully be called 'the Chandler paradigm', is deceptively simple in concept but has powerfully influenced a generation of economists and business historians (Lee, 1990; *21–2*). This study follows recent trends in placing what Chandler has called the rise of 'managerial capitalism', particularly in manufacturing industry, at the heart of its discussion. However, it is important to set this in the context of growing reservations about many aspects of his schema, particularly when attempts are made to extend it beyond the specific cultural context of the United States (see pp. 71–2).[2] Large-scale enterprises in areas other than manufacturing, such as transportation, mining and banking, is also considered, although, as discussed later on, the forces leading to business concentration in these sectors often preceded, and were in some ways different to, those affecting manufacturing.

Two particular difficulties arise in explaining the historical development of big business: defining the terms under discussion and accommodating the diverse experience of corporate growth in different countries and different industries. This survey therefore starts with some definitions, and advances a number of generalisations about the features common to big business in different American and European industries; in particular, the vital role played by railway companies as pioneers of large-scale managerial enterprise. Discussion then turns to the key variations in the timing, degree and form of big business growth. These are of particular significance because much discussion of differing growth rates in the American and western European economies since the 1870s has turned on the structure and management of industry

(Landes, 1969; Elbaum and Lazonick, 1986). The major explanations for the rise of big business are then reviewed, before finally moving to a brief consideration of the welfare implications of the rise of the corporate economy in capitalist societies.

2

The nature and origins of big business

Big business is commonly identified with such images as mono-lithic corporate head offices in London or New York, housing anonymous but powerful bureaucracies, or personified in terms of the wealth-accumulating careers of industrial magnates like Henry Ford, William Lever and Alfred Krupp. These notions may serve to reinforce popular anxiety about giant firms but they have rather limited analytical value. It is therefore important to define the term big business more precisely.

Definitions

Despite growing at different rates and in varying forms between the 1850s and the 1930s, modern, large-scale business corpora-tions in Europe and America shared enough common character-istics to enable the historian to make some very necessary generalisations about their origins and evolution.

1. In the first place, and perhaps rather obviously, big business can be distinguished from traditional enterprise by virtue of its size; it employed far larger capital assets and greatly expanded work-forces. These large enterprises also tended to employ more of their assets in the form of fixed capital, rather than working capital.[3]

2. Big business usually embodied an integration of potentially separate processes or plants. Horizontal integration joined similar or identical firms: for example, combinations of indivi-dual coal mines or breweries. Vertical integration amalgamated different stages in a manufacturing process, between raw

materials acquisition and final product sales: a steel firm might integrate backwards, by merging with coal and iron-ore mining firms; a brewery might integrate forwards, purchasing bars or public houses. Firms frequently engaged in both horizontal and vertical integration, although the latter is regarded as the more significant characteristic of modern corporations (Williamson, 1985; *85–130*). As firms grew in size and produced higher volumes of a commodity, particularly when coupled with vertical integration within single plants, they were commonly able to reduce unit costs; thus achieving 'economies of scale'.

3. Integration of individual business units could be achieved in two major ways: by forming federations between legally separate firms, or by outright merger of those firms into a new and larger company. The first took a complex variety of forms: from informal networks of control represented by interlocking direc-torships in firms; through legal trust devices, which transferred control, but not beneficial ownership, of a group of firms to a parent company; to formal cartel agreements governing such things as prices and market share. In some circumstances, federations offered an alternative to legal merger; in others they constituted an intermediate stage between a competitive market structure and full managerial integration.

4. It was increasingly common, especially during the twentieth century, for business corporations to diversify into new product lines: chemical firms developing new ranges of drugs, synthetic fibres or dyestuffs, for example. Such firms were often charac-terised by their commitment to continuing programmes of scientific research and development (R&D), in order to develop and refine new products. Where companies were able to reduce unit costs through product diversification, perhaps making use of previously under-utilised managerial capacity or bi-products, they can be said to have enjoyed 'economies of scope'.

5. Concomitant to integration and product diversification, big busi-ness normally engaged in multi-plant operation, often diffused over wide geographical areas. Where firms owned and controlled income-generating assets in more than one country, they can be defined as a rather prominent sub-species of big business: multi-national enterprise (Jones, 1986; *2*).

6. As a particular consequence of horizontal integration, coupled with the internal growth of firms, big business was commonly manifested in an increasing market share for leading producers in particular industries. Pure monopoly, in the sense of one firm

controlling total output in an industry, has rarely been experienced in European or American manufacturing and mining, although it has been more common amongst public utilities, such as telephone companies. Instead, it was increasingly common for oligopoly to emerge, where limited numbers of large producers, from two upwards, competed with one another in an industry. Since at least the 1890s, measures of market share have provided one of the more accessible indices of industrial concentration for anti-monopoly legislators in America and Europe, even if such calculations are rather problematic (Hannah, 1983; *179–84*).

7. Where firms grew rapidly, perhaps introducing expensive new technology or sustaining costly R&D programmes, the financial burden often exceeded the personal resources of the original owner-entrepreneurs, or the funds that could be generated from retained profits. Mounting merger bids was also an expensive process. These pressures invariably led to outside finance being sought. In some cases investment bankers provided funds and took a managerial interest, reflecting a prominent role for what Marxist scholars in particular have termed 'finance capital' (Hilferding, 1910). In other cases, capital was raised in stock markets: consequently, the equity in large corporations came to be increasingly diffused amongst large numbers of shareholders. Against this, during the twentieth century, an increasing proportion of corporate stock came to be held by large, institutional investors, such as insurance companies and pension funds, with the implication that new structures of corporate control were being forged (Scott, 1985).

8. The growing size, complexity and geographical spread of modern business enterprise necessitated the introduction of novel and increasingly sophisticated forms of management. Consequently, there evolved a new class of salaried executives, organised in hierarchies of upper, middle and lower management; these hierarchies commonly being divisionalised along functional lines (such as marketing, personnel or finance), or from around the 1920s onwards, along regional or product lines. Managerial hierarchies in large, vertically integrated firms came to assume many of the functions previously performed by competitive forces; for example the pricing and allocation of raw materials and semi-finished goods. In this way, Adam Smith's 'invisible hand' of the market mechanism was increasingly replaced by what Alfred Chandler has termed the 'visible hand' of managerial coordination. For many economists, this internalisation of eco-

nomic transactions defines 'the firm', while a market-firm dichotomy provides the focal point for analysis of the modern corporation (Coase, 1937; Williamson, 1975; Mueller, 1986). However, Daems has implied that a market-federation-firm trichotomy offers a more flexible approach to the historical complexity of business evolution (Chandler and Daems, 1980; *204*).

9. With the ownership of large firms becoming more widely diffused, their managers came to own a diminishing share of the equity. It is therefore possible to talk of the divorce of ownership and control as another delineating feature of big business [Berle and Means, 1932; *1-9*]. In sum, the emerging large-scale 'managerial firms' of the late nineteenth and early twentieth centuries can be contrasted with traditional 'entrepreneurial firms', which were small enough to be personally managed by their owners, perhaps assisted by a few foremen or clerical staff. As this transformation increasingly affected the economies of western Europe and the United States, it is possible to talk of a fundamental shift from a system of proprietorial capitalism to one of managerial capitalism.

It must be emphasised that certain of these characteristics, in isolation, do not necessarily identify firms as 'big business'; a single-plant employer of fifty people, for example, might have a high proportion of his capital in fixed assets, due to the technological nature of the product. Conversely, not all large-scale, managerial firms were multinationals or had developed diversified product lines before 1939.

Alfred Chandler has pointed the way towards a less amorphous description of big business than suggested above. In his view 'modern business enterprise is easily defined [and] has two specific characteristics: it contains many distinct operating units and it is managed by a hierarchy of salaried executives' (1977; *1*). As indicated below, this generalisation is especially valuable in helping us differentiate 'modern' big business from large-scale corporations of an earlier era. Chandler goes further by arguing that, despite inter-country or inter-industry variations, emerging big business in Europe and America shared certain general attributes which were determined by broadly similar forces shaping its growth. He suggests that 'modern' enterprises: (i) 'clustered from the start in industries have certain characteristics', (ii) 'appeared quite suddenly in the last quarter of the nineteenth century' and (iii) 'were [all] born and then continued to grow in much the same manner' (1990; *18*).

Fore-runners of big business

Before examining the evolution of big business after the mid-nineteenth century, it is necessary to comment briefly on earlier examples of large-scale enterprise, primarily to distinguish them from 'modern' business corporations.

It is tempting to regard some of the seventeenth and eighteenth-century joint-stock trading firms, such as the English, Dutch and French East India Companies, as fore-runners of modern big business. The most successful of these, the English Company, operated a number of 'factories' in Asia and had a turnover approaching £2 million a year by the 1740s. According to Chaudhuri, it also evolved a complex managerial structure in response to high levels of uncertainty in its extended field of operations (1978; *19–28, 438–40*). Similar considerations apply in the case of banking, where the international context of financial transactions, coupled with a high risk factor, ensured that a number of European and American banks evolved as highly capitalised multinationals well before the mid-nineteenth century. The Rothschild banking houses of London, Paris and Frankfurt, to take a prominent example, had a joint capital equivalent to $20 million in 1825, and operated a number of branches in Europe, the United States and Latin America (Born, 1983; *53–5*). However, in respect of the trading companies, Williamson has argued that these developments 'were not widely adopted by other firms – and in any event represent very primitive forms of divisionalization' (1986; *132*). It is also important to recognise that management in the East India companies and pre-modern banks was invariably recruited from the ranks of the principal shareholders. Bank ownership and management in particular, tended to be defined in terms of family groups. In addition, the relative simplicity of their organisational techniques before the later nineteenth century ensured that they provided models of limited value to subsequent organisation builders.

There are numerous early examples of large-scale enterprise in manufacturing. One of the most notable was the firm established in Belgium around 1799 by an Englishman, William Cockerill. By the 1830s, this had expanded to the point where, it has been argued, it was the largest integrated and engineering concern in the world. The Cockerill company owned coal mines and iron works, as well as producing textile machinery, steam engines, ships, railway equipment and armaments. It controlled about sixty separate establishments in Belgium, France, Germany, the Netherlands, Dutch Guiana, Spain and Poland. By 1837, the business assets of John Cockerill, the founder's son, were valued at 26 million francs (about $5 million).[4] This enterprise may well have been an early diversified multinational but, like the East India Company, is ultimately differentiated from most modern business corporations in terms of its ownership and management. It is difficult to identify any business concerns in Europe or America prior to the mid-nineteenth century, in which the major proprietors, either individuals like John Cockerill or Corporate bodies of wealthy East India merchants, did not exercise effective day to day control of their firms, as well as formulating longer-term corporate strategy.[5] It must also be recognised that vertical integration, product diversification and multi-plant operation of the type apparent in the Cockerill company, were exceedingly rare before a series of major market transformations between the 1840s and 1870s, which set broad areas of American and European industry on the path towards big business and managerial capitalism.

The key factor in these transformations was technological change in the middle decades of the nineteenth century. On the supply side, innovations in fuel and production technology led the way to higher speed and volume of output in many industries; on the demand side, the development of novel forms of transportation and communication created increasingly integrated national and international markets for these new mass-producers. These developments unlocked a series of constraints on the growth of firms and managerial capitalism (discussed in Chapters 4 and 5), and did so comparatively rapidly. According to Chandler and Daems, 'as late as 1840, there were no middle managers in the United States and very few in Europe . . . nearly all the top level managers were owners, either partners or major stockholders in their enterprises.' However, by the 1920s, 'big business had already become the most influential nongovernment institution in all advanced industrial market economies' (1980; *2–3, 11*).

Railways as pioneers of big business

Construction of the primary railway networks in western Europe and the United States between the 1840s and the 1860s is generally identified as the most significant element in this process, opening up new and expanding markets for the products of agriculture and industry. Rails provided cheaper, faster and more reliable year-round transportation than roads that became quagmires, or rivers and canals which frequently froze, in the winters of the more densely populated regions of north-western Europe and the north-eastern United States. Around 1800, for example, travelling by road between London and Edinburgh, or New York and Pittsburgh (both about 380 miles), could take a week to ten days; by the later 1850s the same journeys by rail took less than a day. Freight rates also fell in Britain and America; from around 12 to 22 US cents a ton/mile by road in the 1830s, to an average of four cents by rail in 1850, and two cents by 1880.[6] Parallel improvements in the cost and speed of ocean shipping helped integrate world markets, especially for an island trading nation like Britain. In this way, transportation developments, and particularly railways, stimulated wide sectors of industry to expand by exploiting previously unavailable economies of scale. However, it has been argued that railways had a more dramatic impact on market widening in America than in Europe, where relatively compact geographical regions were better served by pre-railway modes of transport (Chandler, 1977; *49*); this may help account for the somewhat earlier appearance in Europe of large-scale manufacturers like Cockerill.

Railway companies in America and Europe also assume profound significance in the rise of big business inasmuch as they were themselves the first modern, managerial enterprises. Around 1870, there were virtually no other business organisations operating on such a scale, and none in which managerial hierarchies and the divorce of ownership and control had become so widespread.

Multi-plant operation and managerial capitalism only began to occur in any significant way in mining, manufacturing and retailing during the 1880s and 1890s. Railways led the way in encountering and resolving many of the growth problems subsequently experienced by large-scale organisations in other industries, and this resulted from three related pressures. First, the size and technological complexity of railway systems meant their construction and operational costs were on a scale previously unknown to business enterprise and financial institutions; prompting rapid changes in capital markets. Second, the unprecedented organisational complexities of railway operation stimulated a search for new managerial structures and procedures. Third, they had a level of fixed costs which had serious implications for the competitive conditions within which they operated; encouraging experimentation with cartels and mergers, which in turn meant railways were the first modern industry to experience various forms of governmental anti-monopoly action.

Between the 1850s and the early twentieth century, the leading American and European railway companies were the largest employers and the most heavily capitalised business concerns in the world. As early as 1855, one of the leading American railroads, the Erie, employed 4000 people; in contrast, the Pepperell Mills in Maine, one of the largest American textile firms, rarely employed more than eight hundred workers during the 1850s. By 1891, the Pennsylvania Railroad, the largest in the United States, had 110,000 employees; probably the greatest workforce of any business organisation in the world at that time (Chandler, 1965; *19*; 1977; *204*). The picture was similar in Europe: the leading French railway, the Chemin de Fer du Nord, employed 56,600 people in 1913, while the country's largest manufacturer, the engineering firm Schneider, employed around 20,000 (Caron, 1973; *432*; Daviet, in Pohl, 1988; *70*). As late as 1935, Britain's largest business employer was the London Midland and Scottish Railway, whose 222,000 workers far exceeded the 60,000 domestic workforce of the country's biggest manufacturing employer, Unilever.[7]

Constructing and operating the major railway systems, often thousands of miles in length by the 1870s, with their extensive buildings, rolling-stock and other plant, required an unprecedented level of finance, raised over relatively short periods of time.

In Britain of the 1850s and 1860s, there were few industrial companies with assets of more than $2.5 million, but 19 railway companies in 1850 had each raised capital in excess of $15 million (Gourvish, 1973; *290*). At the same time in the United States, while only a few of the largest textile and ironmaking firms were capitalised at $1 million or more, seven major railroads were capitalised at between $10 million and $35 million. Moreover, whilst the former had accumulated their assets over thirty years or more, the rapid pace of railroad construction necessitated the marketing of some $700 million of railroad securities during the single decade of the 1850s (Chandler, 1977; *90*). A similar distinction could be made of Britain, where fixed assets in railways were equivalent to around $3.2 billion in 1890, a sum equal to that in the whole of manufacturing industry.[8] In many parts of Europe, such as Prussia, where almost 75 per cent of share capital raised between 1850 and 1870 was absorbed by railways, governments played a prominent role in their finance and direction (Landes, 1969; *201*; Vagts, in Horn and Kocka, 1979; *612–15*). However, in the United States and Britain, they were constructed without direct state funding, apart from such assistance as rather generous land-grants in the former. The resulting need to mobilise funds from an increasingly widespread public stimulated the rapid growth of modern stock markets and investment banks between the 1840s and the 1870s, particularly those centred on London and New York (Carosso, 1970; *1–28*; Born, 1983; *41–6*).

Because of their complexity and size, railway companies became the first modern, hierarchical business bureaucracies. Unlike even the largest manufacturing, trading or banking firms up to the 1840s, where the owner-managers were likely to be able to supervise their workforces of a few hundred or less on a personal basis, railway companies in America and Europe had to evolve impersonal procedures for coordinating and monitoring their thousands or tens of thousands of operatives. Ensuring the maintenance of equipment and scheduling flows of traffic over extended railway systems also posed novel difficulties. The result was that between the 1850s and 1870s, pioneering American railroad managers like Daniel McCallum of the Erie company and J. Edgar Thomson of the Pennsylvania followed a variety of routes towards a common goal; moulding formalised managerial hierarchies, based upon clearly defined lines of authority and delegated responsibilities. These structures were usually divisionalised on a regional basis, and further sub-divided into functional departments (such as freight, passengers and telegraphs). At the same time, the complex financial affairs of railroads were monitored by means of new cost accounting techniques, which in turn enabled their executives to engage in more effective strategic planning. In this way, the early generation of railroad managers became the first significant body of professional, salaried managers to appear in the business world (Chandler, 1977; *94–187*). A parallel process occurred in Europe, where British railway companies 'led the way in developing relatively advanced techniques in business management . . . [and] did much to raise the status and augment the role of the non-owning, salaried manager . . . [resulting] in the creation of an executive elite, the first group of "corporation executives" to appear in British industry' (Gourvish, 1973; *290*). Similarly in France, the Chemin de Fer du Nord developed a complex managerial hierarchy, based on functional departments working under a central administration (Caron, 1973; *316–22*).

Railways were essential as test-beds for managerial professionalism and organisational innovation inasmuch as there were few alternative models for expanding business organisations to emulate. As already suggested, banks and early trading companies provided no real precedent; likewise, long-established military hierarchies seem to have had a limited impact on organisation building in British and American business (Gourvish, 1973; *301*; Chandler, 1977; *95*), although their impact appears greater in Germany (Kocka, 1971; *135–43*). Organisational forms developed by the railways were transmitted to other areas of business, through new professional journals and the management schools that emerged from the 1880s and 1890s. They also arose in specific instances through the medium of individuals. One such was Andrew Carnegie, who learnt his craft in the pioneering managerial atmosphere of the Pennsylvania Railroad during the 1850s and 1860s, before moving to the primary metals sector; where application of rigorous accounting and monitoring procedures helped make him the most cost-effective mass producer of steel in the world by the 1880s and 1890s (Wall, 1970). Chandler argues that railways generally provided a less direct input into industrial organisation building in Europe than America, especially where the state took a more active role in the ownership and control of their systems, as in Germany (1990; *254, 413–5*). However, in Britain at least, it is still possible to identify particular individuals acting in a similar way to Carnegie. Eric Geddes of the North Eastern Railway, for example, became an enthusiastic advocate of managerial restructuring in British industry during the interwar period, rescuing the ailing Dunlop Rubber Company on the way, in 1921; another was Felix Pole of the Great Western Railway, who became chairman of Associated Electrical Industries in 1928 (Hannah, 1983; *76–9*).

The third sense in which railways anticipated developments experienced subsequently by other industries, was the extent to which they were burdened by fixed costs. Their massive investment in permanent way – embankments, tunnels and bridges – as well as the huge cost of purchasing and maintaining technologically complex equipment like locomotives, rolling-stock and signalling systems, represented a much higher level of fixed assets than in any other industry before the early twentieth century. In addition, because investors in America and Europe tended to favour the security of fixed-interest bonds or debentures, rather than the less certain dividend potential of ordinary stock, almost all railway companies raised a substantial part of their stock market capitalisation as bonded debt; upon which interest had to be paid, regardless of their financial health. In the United States, the particular severity of this problem is apparent in the rising share of bonded debt in total railroad stock market capitalisation; from 35 per cent in 1867, to 52 per cent in 1890; whilst in Britain, 48 per cent of railway stock was subject to fixed interest repayments in 1870, apart from other loans.[9] The net result was that railway companies found they had very limited scope for reducing rates in the face of competitive market pressures. In the context of calculations that fixed costs averaged two-thirds of total costs, American railroad executives of the 1870s and 1880s entered a series of collusive agreements to fix rates, while some systems merged (Chandler, 1977; *133–44*). In Britain, high levels of fixed costs compromised the ability of railways to behave as competitive market theory dictated and so there was a similar momentum towards consolidation; by 1904, the 14 largest companies (out of more than a hundred) controlled

85 per cent of track mileage and 88 per cent of industry receipts (Cain, 1972; *623*).

In both countries, government action was brought to bear, in order to limit these collusive tendencies. In the United States, where railroads were irredeemably associated in the public mind with the excesses of the 'robber barons' such as Jay Gould and Cornelius Vanderbilt, this action was more explicit, starting at the federal level with the Interstate Commerce Act of 1887. This anti-monopoly sentiment, first aroused in respect of the railroads, was later rekindled against a wider range of industries, including oil and tobacco. In Britain, despite the governments of the time having no monopoly policy as such, the responsible department (the Board of Trade) used its statutory powers to limit collusive activity, for example in forestalling a major railway merger in 1907 (Cain, 1972; *629–31*). In other parts of Europe, such as France, Belgium and Germany, conditions were somewhat different; the main railway networks being increasingly run as state monopolies after about 1870, partly because of their complexity and high fixed costs, and partly because of their military significance.

Spread and clustering of big business

With the conjunction of expanding markets and new organisational forms demonstrated by railroad companies, big business spread rapidly to other industries from the 1880s and 1890s, but clustering in certain sectors; especially food, chemicals, primary metals and transportation equipment. Amongst the 20 two-digit groupings adopted by the US Bureau of the Census to classify manufacturing industry, these four account for a clear majority of the largest 200 industrial firms in the United States, Britain and Germany in the earlier part of the twentieth century. In the United States they accounted for 52 per cent of the top firms in 1917 and 49 per cent in 1930; in Britain 69 per cent in 1919 and 58 per cent in 1930; in Germany 61 per cent in 1913 and 55 per cent in 1929 (Chandler, 1990; *18–23*). Amongst the top French industrials of 1912 (83 firms) and 1937 (84 firms), the situation was similar, with 59 and 61 per cent in these sectors (Lévy-Leboyer, in Chandler and Daems, 1980; *130*). In essence, these were the industries where economies of scale, and gains from vertical integration and greater speed and coordination of production flows, as well as gains from high-volume marketing, were the greatest. Many of them, such as synthetic dyestuffs, were what some economic historians have dubbed the industries of 'the second industrial revolution'. Conversely, as discussed in Chapter 4, those areas where these gains were more limited or, like the textile industry, where most internal economies of scale had been exhausted before the advent of mass markets in the railway age (Hannah, 1983; *9–10*), large firms were much less prominently represented. Textile firms, for example, only constituted two per cent of top firms in America in 1930, while they were somewhat more prominent in Britain and Germany, at around 11 to 12 per cent.

Outside the manufacturing sector, major public utilities like gas, electric power and telephone companies also developed into large-scale managerial enterprises, for similar reasons to the railways. Indeed, with a stock market capitalisation of $3.1 billion and half a million employees in 1937, American Telephone and Telegraph (A. T. & T.) was almost certainly the world's largest firm, operating in a virtual monopoly throughout the United States. Similarly, Cable and Wireless, a 1929 merger of nearly all telegraphic and radio communication systems in the British empire, was the United Kingdom's largest firm, on the basis of its market capitalisation of $2.5 billion in 1937.

Stock ownership and family firms

Notwithstanding the rise of the salaried manager, a feature of business organisation common to virtually all sectors in America and Europe until well after 1939, was a continuing role for family ownership and management, even amongst the largest enterprises. There was a clear trend towards dispersed stock ownership from the end of the nineteenth century, particularly in Britain and America, but in many instances family groups were able to maintain their grip on top management, even where they held a diminishing share of the equity.

With their early reliance on stock market capital, railway companies hastened the trend towards dispersed share ownership. In 1850, one of America's leading textile firms, the Boston Manufacturing Company, had 123 stockholders. Three years later, the New York Central Railroad had 2,445, rising to 54,000 by 1929 (Berle and Means, 1932; *10–13, 107*). In Britain, the North Eastern Railway's shareholders increased from 39,000 in 1886 to 55,000 in 1921 (Irving, 1976; *156–7*). Industrial shares were not generally traded on national stock markets in America and Britain until after about 1885 (Navin and Sears, 1955; Hannah, 1983; *19–20*), but in the following half century the ownership of many large enterprises became increasingly dispersed. In their classic study, Berle and Means charted the extent to which the divorce of ownership and control had progressed in American industry by the early 1930s. The most pronounced example of this trend was A. T. & T., whose 7,500 stockholders of 1900 had increased to 642,000 by 1931, with the largest single holding approximately 0.6 per cent of issued stock (1932, *55, 108, 368*). Analogous data for Europe are not readily available but Hannah suggests that a parallel trend was occurring in Britain, citing an estimate that the mean shareholding in a sample of large companies in the mid-1920s was only £301 ($1460) (1983; *56*).

Against this growing divorce of ownership and control, must be set the continuing importance of family groups in broad areas of European and American industry (Hannah, 1982; Okochi and Yasuoki, 1984). In Britain, amongst innumerable examples, can be cited the managerial domination of W. D. & H. O. Wills (the major constituent of Imperial Tobacco at its formation in 1901) by members of the Wills family (Alford, 1973; *184–5, 240–1*) and the close family control of Courtaulds before 1939 (Coleman, 1969; I: *145, 178*; II: *122, 222*). Lever Brothers was likewise dominated by William Lever; notwithstanding the firm's 187,000 shareholders at the time of his death in 1925, this forceful entrepreneur had maintained control of key voting stock and overall corporate management (Wilson, 1954; I: *46–8, 290*). In general terms, Hannah suggests that 55 per cent of the largest 200 British firms had family board members in 1919; rising to 70 per cent in 1930. However, he does point out that these statistics, of themselves, do not imply any specific form of managerial control (in Chandler and Daems, 1980; *53*). In France, proprietorial capitalism appears, if anything, even more pronounced. Old family firms like Schneider, Pont-à-Mousson and De Wendel were directed by founding dynasties until the 1950s and 1960s (Daviet, in Pohl, 1988; *85–7*), while some newer firms like Renault were family controlled until the 1940s (Fridenson, 1972; *123–4*). In Sweden, the Wallenberg family dominated banking, as well as enterprises like Electrolux, Saab-Scania and S.K.F. (Scott, 1985; *155–6*). Even in Germany, where managerial hierarchies had made a widespread appearance by 1914, many leading firms like Krupp, Siemens and Borsig were dominated by family groups before the Second World War (Siemens, 1957; II: *203, 256*; Kocka and Siegrist, in Horn and Kocka, 1979; *100–9*).

American business also retained pronounced elements of familial capitalism until well after 1939, despite being characterised by Chandler as the 'seed-bed of managerial capitalism' (1977; *498–500*). Extreme examples are Ford, which was almost wholly family controlled after 1907 (Nevins and Hill, 1954; I: *331, 572–3*) and the constellation of business interests held by the Mellon family of Pittsburgh, including Gulf Petroleum (90 per cent owned) and Aluminium Company of America (80 per cent owned) (Berle and Means, 1932; 95). More widespread was what can be labelled 'entrepreneurial enterprise', where controlling family groups shared the increasingly complex administration of their enterprises with hierarchies of middle managers. Such firms included Philip Armour's meat-packing business and the Duke family's American Tobacco Company during the 1880s and 1890s (Chandler, 1977; *381–402*). In general terms, Berle and Means suggested that it was possible for minority groups to maintain effective control over a firm when holding as little as 15 to 20 per cent of voting stock, or through some form of legal device if the holding were smaller. On this basis, they calculated that around 55 per cent of the largest 198 American corporations of 1929 were controlled by minority groups, such as families, while the remainder were under management control (1932; *115*).

Although modern big business in America and Europe had common origins in the railways, and then spread to similar areas of manufacturing, it is clear that this growth was not marked by any simple transition from family firms to managerial firms. Complex varieties of both models co-existed into the latter decades of the twentieth century, just as small-scale companies continued to survive alongside large companies. Indeed, in the view of some writers, the increasing fragmentation of share ownership itself made corporate control possible for smaller minority holdings than would have been the case before 1914 (Prais, 1976; *87–90*). Whether this helped preserve elements of family control or facilitated control by non-managerial minorities, such as institutional investors (Scott, 1985; *39–56*), it is clear that European and American big business exhibited a wide variety of forms as it evolved into the early twentieth century.

3
Variations in the rise and spread of big business

It is apparent that, in many senses, there were marked national differences in the growth of big business before 1939. Chandler and Daems, for example, argue that 'the large modern enterprise, which was common in Germany and the United States before World War I, did not become a major force in the British economy until the 1920s and 1930s and not until after World War II in France' (1980; 3). However, these differences need to be clarified since, as has already been suggested, there are various ways in which to define big business. In particular, comparisons based on assessments of firm size (whether measured by assets, sales or employment) are likely to be of more limited value than those which recognise variations in organisational structure. Nevertheless, it is useful to start with a review of the largest industrial enterprises in America and Europe just before the First and Second World Wars.

The largest industrial firms of 1912 and 1937

It is difficult to rank industrial firms in different countries before about the 1950s; there being no readily available consistent data of company turnover, assets or employment, all of which have been used in postwar global listings. This has led business historians to rely on a variety of non-comparable measures in comparative studies of corporate growth. In an influential study of British big business before 1914, Payne (1967) contrasted leading British and American firms on the basis of nominal capitalisation around 1904. More recently, Chandler has listed leading British, American and German industrials between 1913 and 1953 on the basis of market valuation of issued shares for the former, and gross assets for the latter two (1990; *638–721*).[10]

In order to provide a basis on which to discuss the relative sizes of leading American and European industrial firms before 1939, two data sets relating to the largest companies of 1912 and 1937 were assembled for this study, from capitalisation data and stock market prices reported in the *Stock Exchange Year Book* and the *Economist* (London), the *New York Times* and *Moody's Manual of Industrial Securities* (New York) (Schmitz, 1995). Whilst these sources provide a broadly satisfactory assessment of British, Dutch and American firms, their inadequate coverage of French, German and other European firms has had to be complemented by other sources, including Houssiaux (1958) and Feldenkirchen (in Pohl, 1988). The German data present a particular problem. As with a number of American corporations which were closely owned by a family group, such as Ford, there was no effective public market in the stock of many of the leading German industrials. Consequently, Feldenkirchen's rankings for 1913 and 1938, which have been used here, reflect gross assets and are thus not strictly comparable with those based on market capitalisation. Nevertheless, Tables 1 and 2 present useful snapshots of the relative development of the world's largest industrial firms in the first half of the twentieth century.

Table 1 tends to confirm Payne's contention that leading British industrial firms were smaller than their American counterparts. However, it modifies the implication on the basis of nominal capitalisation, that the largest British company (which he lists as Imperial Tobacco) was 16 times smaller than the largest American (U.S. Steel) (1967; *519, 539–40*). It also appears that the largest British firms were at least as large as the leading German ones, allowing for the differences in the data. It might be further observed that medium-large firms in Britain (those ranking between about 25 and 50) appear somewhat smaller than their German counterparts and noticeably smaller than the equivalent American firms. Elsewhere in Europe, company capitalisation data are not readily available before 1914. However, such figures as exist suggest that leading industrial companies outside Britain and Germany were considerably smaller in scale. The leading French

Table 1 *Largest American, British and German industrial firms, 1912 (median market capitalization of issued equity stock, $ million)*[11]

Rank	United States		Britain		Germany[Assets, 1913]	
1	US Steel	757.2	J & P Coats	300.8	Krupp	142.7
2	Standard Oil (NJ)	389.5	Rio Tinto	143.3	Siemens	121.7
3	Pullman	200.1	Imperial Tobacco	111.2	AEG	112.5
4	Anaconda Copper	177.6	Guinness	109.0	Gelsenk. Bergwerks	96.0
5	General Electric	173.8	Shell Transport & Trading	91.0	Deutsch-Luxemburg	67.6
	...		...		...	
10	American Sugar Refining	109.5	Maypole Dairy	41.7	Hibernia	32.1
	...		...		...	
25	Westinghouse Electric	66.8	Calico Printers'	18.3	Orenstein & Koppel	23.9
	...		...		...	
45	American Locomotive	36.6	Whitbread	8.0	Arenberg	13.3

Table 2 *Leading world industrial companies, 1937 (median market capitalization of issued equity stock, $ million)*[13]

	Firm	Country	Sector	Capitalization
1	General Motors	USA	vehicles	2329.2
2	Imperial Tobacco	UK	tobacco	1603.5
3	Du Pont	USA	chemicals	1589.1
4	Standard Oil (New Jersey)	USA	oil	1547.3
5	General Electric	USA	electrical	1422.1
6	US Steel	USA	metals	1212.3
7	Royal Dutch	Netherlands	oil	1062.1
8	Shell Transport & Trading	UK	oil	921.3
9	Vereinigte Stahlwerke	Germany	metals	831.0*
10	International Nickel	Canada	nickel	829.7
11	Union Carbide	USA	chemicals	775.2
12	British American Tobacco	UK	tobacco	766.7
13	Ford	USA	vehicles	704.9*
14	IG Farben	Germany	chemicals	658.6*
15	ICI	UK	chemicals	646.6
16	Anglo-Iranian	UK	oil	625.4
17	Standard Oil (Indiana)	USA	oil	584.0
18	Lever Bros & Unilever	UK	soap, food	580.5
19	Socony-Vacuum	USA	oil	564.6
20	Gulf	USA	oil	560.4*
21	Texas Corporation	USA	oil	543.1
22	Kennecott	USA	copper	530.3
23	R J Reynolds	USA	tobacco	503.1
24	Standard Oil (California)	USA	oil	501.5
25	International Harvester	USA	engineering	490.8

26	American Tobacco	USA	tobacco	447.6
27	Allied Chemical & Dye	USA	chemicals	446.7
28	Anaconda	USA	copper	407.7
29	Chrysler	USA	vehicles	394.6
30	Eastman Kodak	USA	photographic	394.6
31	Guinness	UK	drink	387.8
32	Procter & Gamble	USA	soap, chemicals	368.5
33	Bethlehem Steel	USA	metals	349.6
34	Courtaulds	UK	textiles	348.3
35	Siemens	Germany	electrical	343.1*
36	Liggett & Myers	USA	tobacco	342.8
37	Westinghouse Electric	USA	electrical	341.5
38	Aluminum Co. of America	USA	aluminium	334.6
39	Distillers	UK	drink	308.8
40	American Can	USA	metal products	302.2
41	Burmah Oil	UK	oil	297.4
42	Unilever NV	Netherlands	food, soap	251.0
43	Pittsburgh Plate Glass	USA	glass	240.5
44	Krupp	Germany	metals, engineering	231.2*
45	American Smelting & Refining	USA	non-ferrous metals	229.8
46	Singer Manufacturing	USA	machinery	226.2
47	J & P Coats	UK	textiles	212.9
48	Phillips Petroleum	USA	oil	209.4
49	American Radiator	USA	engineering	202.0
50	Republic Steel	USA	metals	201.7
51	United Fruit	USA	food	201.0
52	Phelps Dodge	USA	copper	198.7

* gross assets in 1937 (1938 for German firms)

firm Saint-Gobain had a stock market valuation equivalent to $34 million in 1912 (Lévy-Leboyer, in Horn and Kocka, 1979; *452*), whilst one of Italy's top manufacturers, Fiat, had a peak market valuation of $14 million in 1906 (Laux, 1976, *196*).

There was a continuing trend towards large-scale business in America and Europe during the interwar period, and whereas there had only been three industrial firms in the world with capitalisation in excess of $300 million before the First World War, by the eve of the Second there were 40 (Table 2). The United States continued to dominate global big business through the 1930s, its firms occupying two-thirds of the top fifty positions; while leading British firms, particularly the Anglo-Dutch giants Royal Dutch-Shell and Unilever, also consolidated their position amongst the world's most heavily capitalised concerns. Medium-large British firms appear smaller than their American counterparts in 1937, but it is doubtful they were still smaller than those in Germany.[12] Meanwhile, the relatively small size of western European industrial companies outside the core group (Britain, Germany, and now the Netherlands) remained apparent; leading firms like Fiat of Italy (vehicles) had assets of $78 million in 1937, Saint-Gobain of France (glass) $72 million, Nestlé of Switzerland (food) $43 million, and Electrolux of Sweden (electrical goods) $25 million (Moody's Manual, 1939).

The data summarised in Tables 1 and 2 lend general support to the view that British firms lagged behind American firms, in terms of absolute size, throughout the half-century before 1939; the proposition that they were smaller than German firms seems less tenable. An alternative approach to the problem of the relative sizes of American and European firms is suggested by the argument that other things being equal, larger economies will tend to engender larger business organisations; a view consistent with Chandler's stress on the size of the American market as a factor promoting big business there (1977; *498–500*). However, such assumptions are complicated by the fact that many leading British firms were substantially or wholly engaged in foreign business; Rio Tinto operated mines in Spain, for example, while petroleum firms like Shell had no British-based manufacturing operations until after 1945. It is also necessary to bear in mind Hannah's comment that 'more than the United States, Britain considered the world its

Table 3 *Total market valuation of issued equity stock, top 25 industrial firms: United States, Britain, France and Germany, 1912 and 1937 ($ million and percentages of GNP or NNP)*[14]

	1912		1937	
	Total ($m)	% GNP/NNP	Total ($m)	% GNP/NNP
United States	3675	9.3	17,686	19.5
Britain[domestic]	1146	9.2	5906	21.8
Britain	1399	11.2	7662	28.3
France	655	6.3	854	6.4
Germany[assets]	1131[1913]	9.1	3778[1938]	9.6

Britain[domestic] equals firms primarily engaged in domestically-based manufacturing, as defined and listed by Hannah (1983; *102–3, 185–90*).

marketplace, and it exported roughly a third of its output for most of the twentieth century' (in Chandler and Daems, 1980; *62*). This raises the possibility that the domestic British economy is not as appropriate a context for gauging the size of firms as it is in the American case. It also suggests that in such calculations, British firms primarily engaged in domestic manufacturing ought to be assessed separately from the total population of leading industrial firms.

In these terms, Table 3 suggests that in relation to the size of national product, the top 25 American and domestically-orientated British firms were similar in size in 1912, with the possibility that the latter had opened a slight lead by 1937. Inclusion of the leading British overseas mining and oil companies reinforces this view. Table 3 also appears to confirm the smaller relative scale of French business enterprise throughout this period, while the German figures are rather too problematic to reach any particular conclusions. The choice of 25 firms is admittedly an arbitrary one; however, it is unlikely that calculations based on a larger figure would significantly alter the conclusion that leading British firms should not be regarded as 'small' by American or German standards, even before 1914.

A different perspective of corporate growth is provided by estimates of the market share of the top hundred firms in the United States, Britain and France (Table 4). Although these

Table 4 *Net share of manufacturing output of the top hundred firms: United States, Britain and France, 1909/12–1962/3*

	1909	1929	1935	1963
United States	22%	25%	26%	33%
Britain	16%	26%[1930]	23%	38%
France	12%[1912]	16%	—	26%[1962]

(Prais, 1976; *4, 213*; Hannah, 1983; *180*; Daviet, in Pohl, 1988; *73*)

figures are subject to some margin of error, they confirm a general upward trend in business concentration, with possible occasional reversals. They also reflect Britain, and more so France, lagging behind America before the First World War; then Britain rather hesitatingly drawing level with the United States in the interwar period, before emerging as an apparently more concentrated economy in the 1960s. This perhaps confirms Hannah's view that in the 1920s, 'a merger wave and other developments in large corporations . . . marked the birth of the modern corporate economy in Britain' (1983; *7*).

Sectoral distribution of large firms

Not only were there differences between the size and market share of leading American and European firms, there were also some marked variations in the industries in which they were located. It has already been suggested (pp. 16–17) that emerging large-scale companies tended to cluster in industries with similar character-istics; those in which cost advantages arising from enhanced volume and coordination of production flows and marketing were particularly pronounced. This was true of primary metals produ-cers, for example, with the result that in the years around 1912 to 1919, between 15 and 25 per cent of the largest firms in Britain, Germany, France and the United States were clustered in this one sector. However, as indicated in Table 5, there were significant differences in the broader distribution of firms between what are usually termed consumer goods industries (food, textiles etc) and producer's, or capital goods industries (metals, machinery, chemi-cals etc). The predominance of large-scale consumer goods produ-

Table 5 *Sectoral distribution of the largest American, British, German and French industrial firms, 1912/19–1929/30 (percentage)*

	Food, drink, tobacco, textiles (20–22)	Heavy industries (28–29, 33–37)	Other industries
UNITED STATES			
1917	20.5	65.0	14.5
1930	20.0	63.0	17.0
BRITAIN			
1919	45.0	47.0	8.0
1930	44.0	40.0	16.0
GERMANY			
1913	21.0	68.5	10.5
1929	26.5	60.5	13.0
FRANCE			
1912	14.5	77.0	8.5
1929	17.5	73.0	9.5

Data refer to the top 200 firms in the United States, Britain and Germany (Chandler, 1990; *21–3*); for France, the top 83 in 1912 and top 85 in 1929 (Lévy-Leboyer, in Chandler and Daems, 1980; *130*). Figures in brackets are the U.S. Bureau of the Census two-digit, Standard Industrial Classification (SIC) groups; those classified under heavy industry comprise: chemicals, petroleum, primary and fabricated metals, machinery, electrical and transportation equipment; other industries (10 SIC groups) include: apparel, lumber, furniture, paper, rubber and leather.

cers, coupled with a relative unimportance of the heavy sector in Britain is particularly noticeable; while a rather low incidence of large-scale firms in the French consumer goods sector is also apparent. Payne shows that 21 of Britain's 52 largest industrial firms in 1904 were located in food and drink (SIC group 20) (1967; *539–40*). Little changed in the interwar period, with 63 of the leading 200 firms around 1930 concentrated in this sector, compared with 31 in the United States and 28 in Germany. Conversely, only six of Britain's top 200 in 1930 were located in the technologically important non-electrical machinery group (SIC 35), which included such products as turbines, machine tools and office equipment; in both Germany and America the figure was 19 (Chandler, 1990; *21–3*). The extent to which these patterns reflected Britain's position as a premature consumer economy is examined in Chapter 4, as is the suggestion that the continuing prominence of the rural sector in the French economy inhibited the growth of big business amongst its food, drink and textile producers.

A complicating factor in analysing the sectoral distribution of large corporations is the degree to which they developed diversified product lines. This trend is clear within the United States; whereas only three of the top 81 firms of 1909 had 10 or more product lines, by 1935 the figure was 17 out of 82. At the same time, the number of firms with four or less lines was halved, from 66 to 35 (Chandler, 1969; *290–5*). International comparisons are hindered by a lack of suitable data, but on the basis of calculations which he concedes are incomplete, Chandler suggests that only nine of the top 200 industrial firms in Britain around 1930 had four or more product lines; compared with 33 firms in the United States and as many as 61 in Germany (1990; *644–713*). This marked diversification of German firms is confirmed by Kocka and Siegrist, who calculate that nine of the top hundred had 10 or more product lines as early as 1887, rising to 19 in 1907 (in Horn and Kocka, 1979; *80–1*). These contrasts suggest varying potential for achieving economies of scope, as discussed in chapter 4; they also parallel a greater commitment to R&D expenditure in Germany and America than in Britain before 1939 (Mowery, in Elbaum and Lazonick, 1986; *198–222*).

Organizational structures

A dominant theme in studies of big business since the early 1960s has been the proposition that the modern corporation advanced through a number of stages; from the relatively simple owner-managed firms characteristic of mid nineteenth century manufacturing, to the complex, multidivisional organisations which permeate the global economy in the late twentieth century (Chandler, 1962; *7–51*; Williamson, 1985; *273–97*). This structural approach has, in turn, suggested one of the key areas of variation in the growth of large companies during the half century before 1939. Broadly speaking, most scholars argue that whilst a majority of leading firms in the United States and Germany had

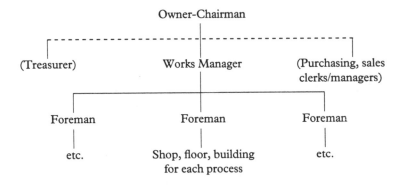

Figure 1 The entrepreneurial firm

adopted new forms of business organisation by 1914, based upon clearly defined hierarchies of professional managers, these innovations had limited impact in Britain before the 1920s and in France before the 1950s (Payne, 1967; *519–39*; Chandler and Daems, 1980; *3–7, 99–105, 118–22*; Hannah, 1983; *7, 22–6*; Chandler, 1990; *11–12*). There are clear dangers in unqualified acceptance of such generalisations since, as suggested above (pp. 17–20), a wide variety of organisational forms existed in European and American big business. Family-dominated management flourished alongside firms led by salaried executives while, in certain circumstances, cartels provided an alternative to integrated corporations. Nevertheless, the Chandler-Williamson models, as described below, do offer a means of discerning patterns in the historical complexity of business evolution.

The authority structure of traditional owner-controlled manufacturing firms, commonly operating a single plant, as described by Chandler (1977; *50–78*) and Pollard (1965; *61–103*), can be characterised as in Figure 1. Even though they were often assisted by works managers, and sometimes by other specialist clerical or managerial staff, individual owners or groups of partners normally took all day-to-day operational decisions as well as setting longer term goals for their firms.

As industrialists expanded the scale and scope of their operations after the 1870s, many adopted increasingly sophisticated organisational structures, in order to control the allocation of resources and

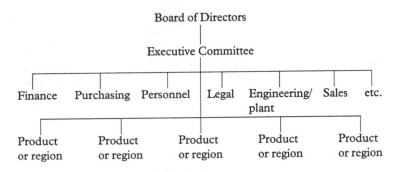

Figure 2 Centralised, functionally departmentalised firm (U-form)

flow of information between the different parts of their firms. The first stage in the evolution of these managerial hierarchies was a functionally departmentalised, unitary structure (U-form), similar to that pioneered in the railway industry, with centralised offices of middle managers responsible for functions like sales and finance (Figure 2). Such structures were adopted by many American firms between about 1890 and 1910, including the American Tobacco Company, Armour and Du Pont (Chandler, 1977; *290–2, 382–402, 438–50*).

By the early decades of the twentieth century, some firms in the United States and Germany which had particularly widespread and diverse operations, suspected they were suffering from growing organisational paralysis; with the centralised control structure of the U-form being increasingly unable either to efficiently monitor the extended functions of management or to separate day-to-day operational decisions from the formulation of longer-term strategy. Consequently, a new decentralised, multidivisional structure, the M-form (Figure 3) emerged; being first adopted in Germany around 1910 by the electrical firm Siemens und Halske (Kocka, 1971; *147–55*), and in America by the chemicals firm Du Pont, during 1920–21 (Chandler, 1962; *91–113*). As noted below, some firms assumed the M-form without having first adopted the U-form. The essential difference between the two was that, with the M-form, managerial control over such functions as R&D and sales was located in each corporate division, which were thus capable, in theory, of operating as separate firms. Whilst upper management were freed to make long-term planning decisions and

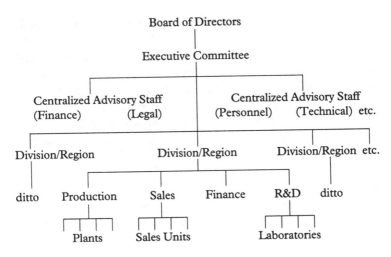

Figure 3 Decentralised, multi-division firm (M-form)

allocate resources throughout the organisation, middle management remained responsible for routine operational procedures within their divisions.

Oliver Williamson warns of the difficulties involved in allocating firms to these categories, and highlights a particular problem arising from consideration of decentralised structures. From around the 1890s, many firms grew in size by acting as holding companies, with controlling interests in a number of subsidiaries. However these types of structure (H-form), as employed by U.S. Steel before 1929 and Imperial Tobacco until 1964 (Chandler, 1962; *333–4*; Alford, 1973; *309–26, 445*), were generally little more than loose combinations of individual business units, with minimal centralised coordination. Williamson therefore differentiates them from the integrated administrative networks represented by the M-form organisation (1986; *61–71, 133*). Indeed, General Motors experienced sufficient difficulty with the H-form organisation it developed in its early years, to move quickly to join Du Pont in adopting an M-form structure, between 1920 and 1925 (Sloan, 1963; *42–115*; Chandler, 1962; *114–61*).

International comparisons of business organisation before 1939 tend to be problematic because the available models, largely generated in the American context, are often inappropriate to

European experience. A case in point is the German chemicals firm I. G. Farben. Created in 1925 by a merger of leading producers including BASF and Bayer, this was a vast decentralised organisation with more than fifty semi-autonomous divisions. However, it does not fit any of the Chandler or Williamson models since, as Hayes notes, it operated very efficiently under a 'flexible system of widely dispersed authority' in which 'decisions were taken at the lowest level possible, and only the most precedential matters percolated upwards' – a system dubbed the 'Habsburg model' within the firm! (1987; *18–19*). There are also conflicting interpretations of some firms' managerial structures. The French company Saint-Gobain, for example, is depicted by Lévy-Leboyer as being led by an innovative hierarchy of professional managers before 1914, who adopted an M-form structure as early as 1905 (in Horn and Kocka, 1979; *452–66*). However, following extensive study of the firm's history, Daviet concludes it was dominated by rather conservative family interests and 'the first hints and references to American patterns of management appeared about 1935' (in Pohl, 1988; *77*). Hannah warns of similar problems in identifying managerial structures in British firms from incomplete sources (in Chandler and Daems, 1980; *52*).

Despite these difficulties, there remain sufficiently pronounced national variations in the assimilation of managerial capitalism to present scholars with a complex problem of historical explanation. Additionally, mirroring this organisational heterogeneity, there was marked variation in the extent to which firms followed strategies of vertical integration or multinational expansion, even within the same industry.

By the First World War, the vast majority of leading industrial companies in the United States and Germany, unlike in Britain, France and other parts of Europe, were vertically integrated and administered by managerial hierarchies. Chandler's listing of the largest American industrial companies of 1917 suggests that, of 257 firms for which information is available, 201 had U-form structures, while only 17 were H-form; and of 267 firms for which relevant data are available, 225 (84 per cent) were vertically integrated to some degree (1977; *503–12*). The German position is uncannily similar, with Kocka and Siegrist indicating that 84 of the top hundred firms of 1907 were vertically integrated (in Horn and

Kocka, 1979; *81*). There is also convincing (if non-quantitative) evidence that German big business, like that in America, embraced managerial capitalism earlier and more enthusiastically than anywhere else in the world (Chandler, 1990; *393–5*). In one important respect, however, the two models of industrial capitalism parted company in the pre-1939 era. In Germany, a strong tradition of inter-firm cooperation and price-fixing agreements emerged; reflected in the number of industrial cartels – as many as 600 by 1911, rising to 2,500 by 1931 (Feldenkirchen, in Pohl, 1988; *116*, *118*). In the United States, on the other hand, where such practices were increasingly frowned upon, especially in the wake of the Sherman Antitrust Act of 1890, the trend was away from price-fixing pools towards oligopolistic competition (Chandler, 1990; *393–5*). A further difference between many German firms and their American and British counterparts was that the former often turned to the leading banks (Grossbanken) in order to finance expansion; thus leading to a greater degree of banking involvement in top management. This role for finance capital varied between firms and, according to Feldenkirchen, tended to decline in significance after 1918 (in Pohl; *139–42*).

In contrast to America and Germany, leading firms in Britain and France, with relatively few exceptions, continued to be characterised by rather loosely-defined forms of managerial organisation, and generally low levels of vertical integration. The evidence on British integration is mixed, Kocka for example arguing that its firms 'appear generally much less fully integrated', while (within the same volume) Hannah suggests that 'in some respects, integration had gone much further by the early 1920s . . . than in the United States' (in Chandler and Daems, 1980; *58*, *105*). However, in the absence of any systematic data, the general weight of evidence points towards a lesser incidence of vertical integration, within firms, than in America or Germany, particularly before 1914 (Payne, 1967; *532–3*; Hannah, 1983; *104*, *122–3*).

In France, it appears only a handful of firms were vertically integrated before 1939; one exception being Renault, which encompassed steel-making as well as automobile, aircraft and armaments production (Lévy-Leboyer, in Chandler and Daems, 1980; *119*). Renault also had a functionally-departmentalised managerial hierarchy by the 1920s; being strongly influenced by American ideas, which Louis Renault had acquired on a visit to Detroit in 1911. However, like Ford, the firm's management was dominated by its autocratic founder, who held 97 per cent of its stock by his death in 1944 (Fridenson, 1972; *70–2, 124, 323–6*). French enterprise was generally dominated by family firms which often went to great lengths to preserve their independence, shunning outside finance or the opportunity of sharing top management with salaried employees (Landes, 1949; *52–3*). Where French manufacturers sought market control, this was invariably achieved through loose-knit confederations, with mutual exchange of shareholdings (Houssiaux, 1958; *236–41*).

British business was similarly committed to what Chandler has termed 'personal capitalism'; with far fewer firms apparently having U-form or M-form structures than was the case in America or Germany before 1939. Instead, a variety of loosely fashioned structures was adopted where entrepreneurs sought greater market control than could be achieved by the myriad private firms in the economy (Hannah, 1983; *16–24*). First, there was a widespread but generally unsuccessful experiment with trade associations between the 1860s and early 1900s. These price-fixing pacts were notoriously hard to police, being unsupported by any specific monitoring structure or system of sanctions. A classic example was the Soap Manufacturers' Association of 1867, which constantly struggled to control its members during its sixty-year life (Wilson, 1954; I: *59–71*). The next stage, cartels, potentially offered more rigorously defined structures and closer monitoring of members' activities. However, British cartels were generally less effective in achieving market control than their German counterparts, since they rarely managed to wed the multitude of interests represented by their different members. Oft-cited examples of cartels in Britain usually include shipping 'conferences', the first of which was the Hangkow Tea Conference of 1879. However, given the specific circumstances of ocean transportation, these shipping cartels were apparently more effective than their land-based equivalent, and by the first decade of the twentieth century such agreements dominated most long-distance shipping routes. Although not technically a cartel, a classic case of an ill-defined loose combination in British manufacturing industry was the Calico Printers' Association, an 1899 grouping of 59 textile-printing firms, controlling 85 per cent of the domestic market. With a board of directors of 84 members, mostly interested in safeguarding the interests of their own firms, and no administrative processes other than what a contemporary called 'government by mass meeting', this combination quickly ran into severe difficulties and was described in 1907 as 'a study in disorganisation' (Payne, 1967; *528*). By 1914, however, a stronger and more centralised managerial structure appears to have emerged in this organisation, as the influence of the original proprietorial managers waned. Despite such problems, cartels and loose combinations of varying degrees of effectiveness remained a prominent feature of many areas of British business into the 1930s.

Formal merger of separate firms generally offered a better chance of achieving administrative coordination than was the case with cartels, although once again, the British experience suggests this was often difficult to achieve in practice. The Salt Union of 1888, with its capitalisation of £3.7 million ($18.4 million) making it the largest British manufacturing company of the time, represented a merger between 64 firms. As a virtual monopoly, it aimed at greater coordination than previously experienced with trade associations. However, a lack of any administrative restructuring, coupled with its essentially defensive nature, like so many other horizontal mergers in Britain before 1939, results in the Salt Union often being cited by economic historians as a classic example of an unsuccessful combination (Reader, 1970; *102–4*). Even the more successful amalgamations, like English Sewing Cotton of 1897 or Imperial Tobacco of 1901, generally failed to use the opportunity to build centralised managerial hierarchies; being more concerned to preserve the family-centred identities of their component firms (Alford, 1973; *258–326*). One of the few late nineteenth century mergers to construct an efficient centralised bureaucracy, was the highly successful textiles multinational, J. & P. Coats. However, this was largely achieved through their German born and trained manager Otto Philippi, and against a background in which members of the Coats dynasty continued to dominate the highest levels of management (Payne, 1967; *529–36*).

There are few unambiguous examples of complex managerial hierarchies and the hiring of salaried top managers in British manufacturing before the First World War, as was the case in firms like Siemens or Du Pont. One was Nobel Explosives, which later became part of the 1926 merger producing Imperial Chemical Industries (I.C.I.). Formed in 1877 by a consortium of industrialists and financiers, and lacking any prior family interests, this firm was professionally managed from the outset and one of its managers, Harry McGowan, later became a guiding influence in the corporate expansion of I.C.I. (Reader, 1970; *31–2, 208–12*; 1975; *474*). Following the First World War, there were widespread attempts at rationalisation and company reorganisation in Britain. However, the majority of these involved horizontal mergers, and did little to significantly move away from the loosely-administered H-form structures that seemed to typify so much of British industry. One example of a firm which did grow as a vertically-integrated enterprise, with a tightly defined, centralised managerial structure, was Anglo-Persian Oil (later Anglo-Iranian, and then B.P.) (Ferrier, 1982; *160–5, 295–349*). Its innovative chief executive of the period 1925–41, John Cadman, vigorously imitated American managerial practices; leading Chandler to describe him as 'one of the few effective British organization-builders' of the era (1990; *301*). In addition, one or two firms made tentative moves in the direction of M-form hierarchies during the interwar period; most notably I.C.I., which was partly influenced by its commercial links with Du Pont and I. G. Farben (Reader, 1975; *70–97, 127–44*; Hannah, 1983; *81–6*).

If there was marked variation in the adoption of managerial hierarchies and vertical integration, which reflects badly on British entrepreneurs, their response to the possibilities of overseas expansion shows them in quite a different light. Britain's industrialists were particularly prominent in a broad-based expansion of European and American multinational enterprise (MNE) which occurred between the 1860s and 1930s. Counting firms which had manufacturing operations in at least five foreign countries by 1939, Franko identifies 60 subsidiaries established from Britain before 1914; compared with 122 American examples and 167 from other European countries. Between 1914 and 1938, the British firms set up 244 more subsidiaries, while the Americans and Europeans established a further 685 and 412 (1976; *10*). A notable example is Lever Brothers, which by 1902 operated manufacturing subsidiaries in Australia, Canada, the United States, Germany and Switzerland, as well as copra plantations in the Pacific (Wilson,

Table 6 *Stocks of American and European foreign direct investment,*
1914–83; in 1938 prices ($ billion)

	1914	1938	1983
United States	4.2	7.3	12.5
Britain	10.2	10.5	5.3
France	2.8	2.5	1.7
Germany	2.4	0.35	2.2

Derived from estimates in Dunning, 1988; *74*

1954; I; *98, 160*). It is important, however, to recognise that not all
multinationals were large-scale enterprises and many operated
only one foreign venture (Jones, 1986; *3–4*).

The geographical spread of British MNE was also wider, and
represented a greater volume of investment, than that from any
other nation before the Second World War. Whilst American
MNE largely reflected what Mira Wilkins has termed the 'spillover'
into Canada and Latin America, (1970; *110*; 1974; *55, 182–3*), and
continental European MNE was concentrated within Europe
(Franko, 1976; *47, 86–92*), British MNE was rather more cosmo-
politan[15] – partly mirroring the extent of its imperial connections
(Jones, 1986; *16–17*). Additionally, British foreign direct investment (FDI) far exceeded that of other nations, although it grew
less rapidly during the interwar period than American investment
(Table 6). It is also worth noting that overall real FDI levels in the
early 1980s appear only marginally higher than those of 1914 and
1938.

Mergers and internal growth

Firms can expand the scale and scope of their operations through
internal growth, by merging with other firms, or a combination of
the two. Despite problems with the data, the broad dimensions of
merger activity since the late nineteenth century have been quanti-
fied (Figure 4), and the results suggest that the relative significance
of mergers and internal growth has varied considerably in different
economies and industries.

Figure 4 Merger activity: United States, Britain, Germany and France, 1895–1939 (firm disappearances – log scale)

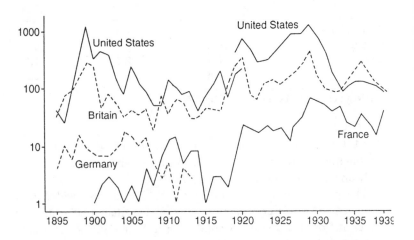

(Nelson, 1959; *37, 166–7;* Hannah, 1983; *175–6;* Houssiaux, 1958; *340;* Tilly, 1982; *635.*) The break in the American series at 1919–20 reflects a change in the method of calculation and although it does not significantly alter the general pattern of activity, the earlier series understates the total number of mergers, such that on the later basis the 2,653 disappearances of 1898–1902 would have risen to over 8,400 (Nelson, 1959; *25–9*).

Pre-1939 merger statistics exhibit three noteworthy features. First, allowing for some differences in the way the individual series were compiled, it appears that America and Britain experienced consistently higher levels of firm absorption than Germany or France. During the decade 1904–13, for example, the United States saw 1,031 firms disappear in mergers, against 427 in Britain, 96 in Germany and 55 in France; although it is apparent that the American and French figures are under-estimates before 1919 (Nelson, 1959; *25–9;* Houssiaux, 1958; *339*). Secondly, apart from brief divergences, there appears to be a broad correlation between the individual series, particularly the American, British and French; suggesting the influence of related forces. Thirdly, there were three particularly pronounced merger waves during this period; around 1898–1902, 1919–20 and 1926–30.

The relatively low level of French and German merger activity confirms a general belief that internal growth was far more influential in their pre-1939 business concentration than was the case in Britain or America. Houssiaux argues that French firms had a preference for internal expansion and while there were some significant fusions, for example that which created the chemicals combine Rhône-Poulenc in 1928, mergers were of limited significance before 1945 (1958; *289–375*). Similarly, Tilly calculates that mergers accounted for no more than a fifth of overall growth in a sample of German industrial firms between 1880 and 1913. Again, merger was important in creating specific combines, most notably the Siemens-Schuckert and AEG fusions of 1903–4, but these were very much the exception (1982; *634–42*).

Whilst mergers were more prominent in Britain and America, there has still been some debate about their contribution to increasing business concentration. Berle and Means, for example, calculated that 81.5 per cent of the asset growth of America's 200 largest firms between 1922 and 1927 arose through internal growth (1932; *43*). Against this, Nelson expressed a more widespread view when he suggested that 63 of the 100 largest industrials of 1955 experienced their major spurt of growth as a result of merger activity; including 20 in the 1895–1904 wave (1959; *4*). The prime importance of the turn-of-century merger movement in shaping many leading American firms is supported in a recent study by Lamoreaux, although she argues many of these early consolidations proved incapable of retaining control of their markets in the longer run (1985; *138–58, 187*). The British position is perhaps less clear-cut, with Prais arguing that mergers are no more important than other factors in explaining concentration (1976; *92, 125–6, 134, 279–80*); while Hannah contends that they were the major force in the rise of big business. Taking issue with Prais, he calculates that more than 75 per cent of the increase in market share of 600 leading firms between 1919 and 1930 is accounted for by mergers. He also concludes that the amalgamation movements of the 1920s enabled British firms to make up much of the ground lost to the American firms which had expanded during the pre-1905 merger wave (1983; *92–9, 228–9*).

Merger activity appears to have been particularly important to the growth of firms in those sectors which dominated big business before 1939, including food and drink, chemicals and primary metals (p. 23 above). In the United States these three SIC groups, together with transportation equipment, accounted for 53 per cent of manufacturing absorptions between 1895 and 1920 (Nelson, 1959; *42*). In France, the same three, plus the 'machinery' sector, accounted for more than 71 per cent of disappearances in manufacturing between 1900 and 1955 (Houssiaux, 1958; *341*). The British picture is less clear, but Hannah's sample of mergers in the 1920s shows that mergers were similarly prominent in chemicals, food, shipbuilding and metals (1983; *98*). Thus, whatever differences there may have been in the overall significance of mergers to corporate growth, the evidence suggests that firms in these industries found similar advantages in external growth strategies.

4
Institutional and technological factors in the rise of big business

Innumerable theories have attempted to account for the growth of big business. Of these, almost certainly the oldest and most pervasive identifies a universal desire amongst entrepreneurs for market control and monopoly profits as sufficient explanation of increasing business concentration. As early as 1776, Adam Smith recognised this trait when, in a much-quoted passage, he declare: 'People of the same trade seldom meet together, even for merriment and diversion, but the conversation ends in a conspiracy against the public, or in some contrivance to raise prices.'[16] Such has been the impact of Smith's vision of perfectly competitive markets ensuring optimal economic coordination and resource allocation, according to Chandler, that much economic theory has approached large-scale enterprise with profound suspicion and has taken little trouble to search far beyond the market control motive (1977; *4*). A desire to minimise competition undoubtedly lay behind a considerable part of pre-1939 merger activity and cartelisation (Lamoreaux, 1985; *6–8, 108–9*; Maschke, 1969; *227–8, 240–1*). However, as Hannah points out, precisely because entrepreneurs have probably always had this motive in mind, it has limited historical significance, in isolation, in explaining growing business concentration since the late nineteenth century – whether this occurred through firms or federations (1983; *5–6*). Other influences, particularly institutional, technological and market factors, must also be considered in order to explain the great diversity as well as the general trends apparent in the evolution of big business.

Institutional factors

Institutional influences on business concentration include the structure and functioning of capital markets, and the role of government, as well as patterns of social and cultural values in different countries. It is also convenient to summarise Marxist perceptions of big business in this section, since they tend to focus on some of these themes.

Capital markets

Access to capital is widely regarded as influential in the growth of firms, and the manner in which financial institutions – banks and stock markets – fund business expansion is seen as a key explanation of variations in the development of big business. Nevertheless, for much of the nineteenth and twentieth centuries the principal sources of business finance in Europe and America were retained earnings and funds provided by family and partnership groups (Best and Humphries, in Elbaum and Lazonick, 1986; *224*). Where firms could accumulate capital over extended periods, self-finance was usually sufficient to fund expansion. This was particularly the case in Britain and France, where many firms in traditional industries like textiles or metal-working were able to grow to considerable size without recourse to outside funding, whilst maintaining the controlling interest of family or partnership groups (Cairncross and Hunter, 1987; Lévy-Leboyer, in Chandler and Daems, 1980; *124*). In contrast, where firms grew rapidly, moved into capital-intensive technologies or engaged in costly merger activity, external funding often became necessary, at least to the point where increased income flows enabled them to reduce this dependence.

A complex set of arguments relate capital markets to business concentration. In the British case, debate ranges from the view that financial institutions ignored the needs of domestic industry, particularly in new high-risk technologies (Kennedy, 1987), to the suggestion that stock markets channelled funds too readily into small firms, thus perpetuating an atomistic and excessively competitive structure in British industry (Best and Humphries, in Elbaum and Lazonick, 1986; *225*). In parallel terms, British and French stock markets, well-attuned to industry's needs, have been contrasted with their less well developed counterparts in Germany, where firms found it harder to raise capital through security issues (Michie, 1988; Tilly, 1982; *644–50*). Consequently, there was far greater German reliance on bank funding, although this diminished after the First World War, partly as a result of increased self-financing. Similarly, Davis (1966) contends that late nineteenth-century American financial markets were less well developed than Britain's, so that access to external funds, particularly bank finance, helps explain the concentration of business power in the hands of men like Carnegie and Rockefeller. However, Chandler argues that privileged access to capital was generally unimportant in the growth of leading American corporations; instead it was the larger, internally-generated cash-flow which some firms achieved through integrated production and marketing (1977; *373*). In broader terms, fairly close positive correlations between stock price movements and merger activity in America, Britain and Germany between around 1880 and 1918, suggest that financial factors were not unimportant in determining the pace of business concentration (Tilly, 1982; *651*; Nelson, 1959; *89–100*).

The role of banks in promoting business concentration has been a particular focus of attention since Hilferding advanced his finance capital thesis (1910). In this view, bankers are seen as influencing client firms to pursue growth strategies, so as to consolidate their investments, spread the risk over a wider range of activities and reap the promoters' profits possible from mergers (Scott, 1985; *22–56*; Prais, 1976; *92–100*). However, the evidence here is mixed. By 1905, the eight leading German Kreditbanken held 819 directorships in client firms; there is also evidence that they had a bias towards funding heavy industry and large-scale capital users (Neuburger and Stokes, 1974; *710–29*). In the American case, the extent of bank influence over industry seemed to be confirmed by the findings of a 1912–13 Congressional investigation (the Pujo commission) which calculated that 180 directors from an 'inner circle' of banks served on the boards of 341 leading industrial corporations, with combined assets of $25 billion (Carosso, 1970; *137–55*). Bankers like J. P. Morgan and Kuhn

Loeb were also heavily engaged in pre-1914 merger funding, the rewards often being immense (the Morgan syndicate received $50 million for underwriting the U.S. Steel flotation in 1901) (Carosso, 1987; *473*). On the other hand, Neuburger finds little to support the view that German banks were dominant in their relationship with industry. In many cases, such as the Deutsche Bank links with Siemens and AEG, the latter had the upper hand (1977; *191–207*). Additionally, Carosso argues that the Pujo commission failed to demonstrate that the bankers were able to effect a reduction of competition amongst these firms (1970; *151–2*). He also suggests that the influence of the Morgan banking house varied considerably amongst its clients and tended to decline over time (1987; *486–91*).

It appears difficult to generalise about the role of financial institutions in promoting big business, particularly in view of increasing internal funding; a trend confirmed after about 1920 by the evolution of M-form organisations, which Williamson has described as taking on many of the properties of internalised capital markets (1985; *281*). Against the declining role of bank finance, however, must be weighed the growth of institutional investment, although this did not become particularly significant until after 1939 (Prais, 1976; *117*; Scott, 1985; *68*). There is also a deeper problem inasmuch as it is unclear whether specific financial institutions functioned as a cause or effect of differing business environments. Thus, in the British case, relatively weak capital market-industry relations may have been a consequence rather than a determinant of the slower growth of large firms (Collins, 1991; *93–7*).

The role of government

Whilst capitalist governments played a generally negligible role in macroeconomic management between the 1850s and 1930s, they still impinged upon business concentration in a variety of ways; as entrepreneurs in their own right, as customers of industry, and as legislators moulding the business environment. In parts of nine-teenth-century Europe, they also provided firms with models of bureaucratic organisation (p. 21 above).

Direct state ownership of industry was rare in western Europe and America in the century before 1939, despite a venerable interventionist tradition in the former (Landes, 1969; *129–39*), and was almost wholly confined to public utilities or transportation systems in which 'natural monopolies' appeared to exist.[17] Continental European nations frequently operated their railways as state monopolies (p. 23 above), while Britain's telephones and the larger part of its electricity generating capacity were operated by central or local government after the 1880s (Hannah, in Nakagawa, 1980). Governments also frequently influenced the growth of firms supplying strategically vital products, particularly armaments manufacturers like Krupp and Schneider. In Britain, this was evidenced in the government sponsored Vickers-Armstrong merger of 1930, when its two major armaments suppliers were threatened by poor management records and contracting markets (Scott, 1962; *144–89*). The need to secure naval fuel supplies also led the British government into taking a majority stake in the Anglo-Persian Oil Company on the eve of the First World War; an involvement which the firm's historian regards as vital in understanding its innovative approach to management and business strategy in the interwar period (Ferrier, 1982; *10–11*). On a broader front, the exigencies of the Great War prompted widespread state intervention in European industry, although in most cases wartime controls were hastily dismantled after 1918 (Nakagawa, 1980; *112–13, 144–6*). This was especially true of Britain, leading Hannah to conclude that the state played no significant role in the framing of the business environment, particularly as far as manufacturing industry was concerned (1983; *41–53*). In contrast, closer relationships between industry and government (and banks) in Germany, have prompted Kocka (in Chandler and Daems, 1980; *107–10*) to explain this along Gerschenkronian lines, as a case of institutional substitution, reflecting the country's relative 'lateness' in industrialisation, compared with Britain and France.[18]

The legislative impact on big business was most apparent in respect of tariffs, patents, corporation law and anti-monopoly policy. From the vantage point of a Britain that remained committed to free trade until 1932, high levels of tariff protection in America and continental Europe often seemed to explain relative differences in the success of cartels and combinations (Payne, 1967; *526*). In the German case there is considerable support for the view that increasing tariffs after 1879 facilitated vertical integration and cartelisation, particularly in heavy industry (Kocka, in Chandler and Daems, 1980; *107*; Webb, 1980). However, the picture is less certain elsewhere. Wohlert suggests that Swedish tariffs of 1882 and 1892 had a mixed effect on concentration (in Pohl, 1988; *46*), while Chandler argues that American protectionism favoured industries that remained competitive just as much as those which became concentrated (1977; *374*). Hannah also argues that protectionism played a minor role in British corporate growth during the 1930s (in Chandler and Daems, 1980; *60–1*). Against this, rising tariffs appear to have been a significant factor in the growth of American and European multinational enterprise (Caves 1982; *40–3*).

Patent law appears to have had a similarly uncertain effect on business concentration. Many firms clearly benefitted from privileged access to new technology, an example being the tobacco firm W. D. & H. O. Wills, which grew to dominate British markets after 1884 largely on the basis of its exclusive U.K. rights to the new Bonsack cigarette machine (Alford, 1973; *139–57*). However, in the American case, Chandler argues that while patents may have aided the growth of some firms, like Bell telephone, such advantages were generally transitory; instead, ongoing commitment to R&D provided a more effective growth strategy (1977; *200–3, 374*). This was perhaps most impressively witnessed before 1939 in the case of Du Pont, which developed a wide range of new products including synthetic fibres, dyestuffs and drugs (Hounshell and Smith, 1988).

Opinions also differ about the impact of corporation law and anti-monopoly policies on the growth of big business. Legislation permitting modern joint-stock, limited liability incorporation appeared in America, Britain, France and Germany around the same time during the 1850s and 1860s, but was too similar to allow any simple conclusions to be drawn about its effect on variations in business concentration (Horn and Kocka, 1979; *124–85*). On the other hand, there appears a clear contrast between the antitrust policies pursued in the United States from the 1870s and the more favourable treatment of cartels in Europe. At one extreme,

German law seems to have increasingly encouraged market-fixing agreements, through a series of favourable court decisions such as the Saxon Wood Pulp Cartel case of 1897, to compulsory cartelisation in many industries during the Nazi regime of the 1930s (Feldenkirchen, in Pohl, 1988; *115–19*). However, despite the views of Marxist historians, it is unwise to characterise the German state as consistently promoting the interests of big business. In the 1930s, for example, Nazi ideology was simply too ambiguous and frequently displayed hostility towards industrialists (Turner, 1985; *60–71, 181–91, 328–39*). French and British law also broadly supported the legality of cartels and trade associations, especially from the 1880s onwards (Keller, in Horn and Kocka, 1979; *517–19*).

In America, by way of contrast, marketing-fixing agreements were increasingly curtailed by state and federal legislation, although there is continuing debate about the impact of these policies. Despite some notable successes, such as the enforced break-up of Standard Oil in 1911, it has been argued that the Sherman Antitrust Act of 1890, and its subsequent interpretation in a series of Supreme Court decisions, actually promoted the growth of big business by encouraging the abandonment of cartels in favour of large, integrated firms. Meanwhile, in Europe, the lack of such constraints perpetuated a regime of smaller firms which tended to seek market control through federations (Chandler, 1977; *331–4, 375–6*). However, this view has been criticised from at least two directions. Sklar suggests that until 1897, prevailing interpretations of the Sherman Act were no less favourable to cartels than was British law (1988; *157–63*). Hannah also rejects a simple link between antitrust law and concentration, which might be tenable with an American-British comparison but falls down when Germany is brought into the picture, arguing that the latter achieved higher concentration than Britain before the 1920s when pursuing more overtly pro-cartel policies (in Horn and Kocka, 1979; *311–12*). In this context, though, it is worth recalling comments about the relative sizes of British and German firms before 1914 (pp. 29–34 above).

A broader perspective of the apparent failure of American antitrust policy to retard the growth of big business is provided by a number of writers. Kolko, in a Marxist interpretation, suggests that industrialists influenced the framing of antitrust policy before 1917, so as to obtain statutory quasi-cartel arrangements (1963; 1965), although this view has been criticised, amongst others, by Martin (1971) and Lamoreaux (1985; *162, 171–2*). Internal contradictions in antitrust policy have also been highlighted; as has the constitutional division of authority between the states and federal government, and within the latter between the presidency, congress and the Supreme Court, coupled with a prevailing fear that the only alternative to big business was 'big government', equally antipathetic to the American political tradition (Lamoreaux, 1985; *190–1*; McCraw, in Nakagawa, 1980; *188–206*). Additionally, during the First World War and much of the depression of the 1930s, federal government effectively ignored antitrust law, in order to stimulate the economy (Hawley, 1966).

Recent research points towards the general conclusion that legal systems had no major influence on the growth of big business in Europe or America (Horn and Kocka, 1979; *21–2*). Indeed, Sklar suggests that the determinants of corporate growth 'lie somewhere outside the realm of judicial construction, and, rather, in the realm of property and market relations and of politics' (1988; *163*). It is, therefore, perhaps more useful to consider the wider influence of governments upon socio-cultural values, for example through patronage of the educational system, although (as discussed below) these factors are notoriously difficult to delineate.

Marxist viewpoints

Hilferding's finance capital concept is particularly prominent in Marxist analysis of big business although, from Marx onwards, debate has also extended to technological and labour market considerations, as well as supposed pro-business policies pursued by capitalist governments. Marxist labour market analysis does offer something in terms of originality; regarding the large-scale corporation as a device to control the work-environment and minimise workers' wages (Marglin, 1974).[19] However, its consideration of technological factors appears to differ little from that adopted by mainstream liberal writers. Whilst evidence on the role of banks and governments in promoting big business is ambiguous, as indicated above, Marxist writing has developed its discussion of financial factors in the following terms. Big business strives to maximise profits and with its growing ability to control markets there is a chronic tendency for its 'surplus' to rise. So, a concerted effort is made to absorb this, through such devices as capital export and imperialism (Lenin, 1917; Baran and Sweezy, 1966).[20] It might also be directed into new fields, thus extending networks of corporate control; an example being the channelling of vast oil industry profits by J. D. Rockefeller and his associates into railroad, copper and steel amalgamations in the late 1890s (Nevins, 1940; II: 395; Carosso, 1970; 45). However, the significance of these investment networks is just as difficult to establish as that involving banks, and even Marxist scholars have challenged simplistic theories linking big business with excess profits (Semmler, 1982).

Social and cultural values

Socio-cultural values undoubtedly influence business environments but specifying their impact is complicated by the subjective nature of many of the concepts involved, such as 'traditionalism'. Nevertheless, it is possible to outline the main ways in which these value systems appear to have influenced the growth of big business.

The apparently slow growth of integrated, managerial firms in Britain and France has been widely identified with the persistence of social structures and attitudes antipathetic to corporativist business organisation. Many writers, such as Wiener (1981) and Checkland (in Nakagawa, 1977; 55–72), have discussed the supposed survival in Britain of a 'landed-aristocratic' ethos, which meant, amongst other things, that American and German organizational innovations were often negatively received. Wiener, in particular, has developed such a thesis to the point of suggesting that British society has been plagued, from around the later nineteenth century onwards, by a deep-rooted 'anti-business' culture. In these terms, the dominance of landed-aristocratic values is seen as having been reinforced by a 'traditionalist' educational system, in prompting a much-discussed haemorrhage of entrepreneurial talent from industry to politics, land-owning and the service sector

(Habakkuk, 1962; *190–1*; Payne, 1988; *24, 56*). Wiener's ideas, and wider notions of an anti-business culture in Britain, have come under sustained attack in recent years, most tellingly in the work of Rubinstein (1993). Nevertheless, there clearly remains considerable scope for further research and debate in this highly charged area, especially on a comparative basis, since many of the implied links between anti-business values and managerial conservatism have been identified as much within the French historical experience as in the British. Linked with this argument is the equally contentious view that the prevalence of family-centred firms limited opportunities for corporate growth; the latter commonly appearing to place a premium on perpetuating internal financing and control (Landes, 1969; *131, 209–10, 336–9*; Payne, 1988; *43*). Against this, it is clear that family-dominated management was not incompatible with dynamism and growth, as evidenced in firms like Courtaulds and Pilkington (Hannah, 1982, *3–4*; Payne, in Okochi and Yasuoka, 1984; *171–97*). It is also worth bearing in mind Alford's comment that some entrepreneurial talent could usually be found amongst the large number of sons frequently fathered by businessmen until the interwar period (1973; *240*).

In contrast, American socio-cultural values appear to have favoured corporate growth in a variety of ways. Numerous studies stress the absence of a legally-privileged, business-despising elite in the United States; reflected in an entrepreneurial population less likely to be impeded by conservative mores or attracted to alternative professions (Habakkuk, 1962; *113–14*). European visitors frequently saw 'over-assertiveness' in the American character; according to Cochran, a trait which provided 'a good set of qualities for business success' (in Nakagawa, 1977; *114–19*). This clash of cultures is perfectly illustrated in the offence taken by the Player brothers in Britain, when the leading American tobacco manufacturer arrived in 1901, introducing himself with 'Hello Boys, I'm Duke from New York, come to buy your business' (Alford, 1973; *258*). Although partially tempered by Jeffersonian agrarian-individualism (see p. 76 below), such aggressive self-confidence, a facet of the American vision of 'manifest destiny', undoubtedly aided the process of ostentatious wealth-accumulation as well as technological and organisational innovation.

It has also been argued that American society was characterised by a greater degree of flux and uncertainty than European society; primarily a function of ethnic intermixing and geographical mobility in a rapidly growing population (Cochran, in Nakagawa, 1977; *115–28*) A consequence, Sklar suggests, was that 'the incomparably greater "impersonality" of the market in the United States . . . in contrast with Old World conditions, critically weakened the discipline of deference and honour. Handshakes counted for little and even contracts could often be disregarded or broken with impunity' (1988; *164*). Thus, America came to rely on judicial processes much more than European societies, where informal understandings were more likely to be honoured. This was reflected in relative numbers of lawyers: fifteen per 10,000 population in the United States around 1900, compared with six in Britain and as few as four in France.[21] In these circumstances, costs associated with making contracts may have appeared a more significant element in American business life, compared with Europe, producing a greater incentive to internalise transactions within firms (as discussed in Chapter 5). This therefore suggests a reason, other than the impact of antitrust policy, why American business increasingly abandoned cartels and pooling agreements, unlike their European counterparts.

Germany seems to stand somewhat apart from both the American and Franco-British patterns, largely because pre-industrial militaristic and bureaucratic traditions survived to become key components of political and business culture until the end of the Nazi era (Kocka, 1971; *133–7*). This was evident in an apparently smoother transition to corporativist structures than elsewhere; organisational innovation within firms being embraced more readily than in Britain, whilst a community of interest between business and the state emerged, of a type totally alien to United States experience. In the pre-1939 German context, 'social, cultural and political traditionalism', as well as 'a deep-rooted desire for order', seem to have been generally advantageous to continuing bureaucratisation and the growth of big business (Kocka, in Nakagawa, 1977; *157–66*; Jaeger, in Nakagawa, 1980; *129–49*).

There is widespread agreement that it is difficult to disentangle cause and effect when examining relationships between socio-cultural values and the business system; Habakkuk, for example, asking if 'the abundance of entrepreneurial talent in the U.S.A. was the consequence rather than the cause of a high rate of [industrial] growth' (1962; *213*). Chandler also implies that while entrepreneurial ability might be a useful explanation of general trends in American business concentration, in isolation it can hardly explain the clustering of giant firms in certain industries. 'The most brilliant industrial statesmen or the most ruthless robber barons were unable to create giant multinational companies in the furniture, apparel, leather or textile industries', he states (1977; *373*). It is therefore important to heed Thomas Cochran's warning that 'socio-cultural differences are obvious, colourful, often superficial and easy to exaggerate' (in Nakagawa, 1977; *139*). It might further be observed that cultural values do not only influence broadly defined business environments, but also appear to mould relationships and decision-making processes within firms. Coleman, for example, argues that business organisations may be powerfully influenced by 'inherited attitudes and traditional practices . . . their historically dominant "cultures" ' (1987; *153*).

Markets, technology and economies of scale

The growth of markets, technological change and related possibilities for increasing economies of scale, have long been regarded as a key set of explanations for the development of big business. As Adam Smith suggested in his *Wealth of Nations*, the division of labour (specialisation of tasks), and therefore the potential for mass production and economies of scale, can be seen as being limited by the extent of the market. In these terms, market-widening transportation improvements in the mid nineteenth century have been identified as a key factor enabling business concentration (see pp. 10–11 above). Before the railway age and the advent of rapid, year-round communications, argues Chandler, growth in demand had been largely met by increasing specialisation amongst firms and a corresponding multiplication of producers and distributors. Thus, in *The Visible Hand*, he describes an increasingly fragmented business world in early nineteenth century America; an era when firms 'remained small and personally managed because the volume of business handled by even the largest was not yet great enough to require the services of a large permanent managerial hierarchy' (1977; *48–9*). By the 1870s and 1880s, however, expanding markets were stimulating a continuing quest for high-volume manufacturing technologies as well as an increasing internalisation of production and distribution activities within firms.

Before discussing technology and economies of scale, it is worthwhile examining the influence of expanding markets on business concentration. Between 1850 and 1913 America's population quadrupled, from 23 to 97 million, while Germany's and Britain's grew less rapidly, from 34 to 67 million and 28 to 46 million respectively. In contrast, French population was virtually stagnant, only expanding from 36 to 40 million. There were also increasing contrasts in potential spending power: American per capita G.D.P. (in 1913 prices) rising from $201 in 1870 to $477 in 1913, compared with increases from $255 to $392 in Britain, $165 to $309 in France, and $141 to $282 in Germany. [22] At one extreme, these figures illustrate the dramatic expansion of the American domestic market; at the other they suggest more limited potential for the growth of mass consumption in France and Germany. A pointed example of the extent to which a mass market for consumer goods developed in the United States is provided by automobile ownership: by 1926, it had 164 passenger cars per thousand population, compared with 15 in Britain, 13 in France and just three in Germany.[23] Chandler argues that such a rapidly growing market provided American industrialists with a wider range of opportunities to exploit economies of scale and scope than elsewhere in the world before 1939. He also suggests that a more widely dispersed population, compared with Europe, helps explain why American firms tended to invest more in multiple production and distribution units (1990; *51–2*).

A number of qualifications appear necessary when comparing American and European markets. Hannah argues that in some respects Britain, more highly urbanised than America, was a better potential market for mass products in areas like electrical goods; although he does suggest that demand for mass-produced consumer goods may have been inhibited by lower wage levels. He also argues that domestic market size may not provide apt comparisons, since British industry depended so much more on foreign trade than America or Germany (in Chandler and Daems, 1980; 61–3); a viewpoint reinforced by the fact that British firms engaged in more foreign direct investment before 1939 (p. 41 above). Additionally, it is clear that pre-railway transportation systems more effectively integrated national and regional markets in western Europe than in the sparsely settled North American continent (Chandler, 1977; 49). Against this, poorly developed pre-1914 German markets (a function of relatively low incomes and a widely dispersed population) may have encouraged the pronounced diversification of its industry (see p. 33 above); this quest for economies of scope being seen by Kocka as a risk-minimising strategy in the face of market uncertainty (in Chandler and Daems, 1980; 107–10). The limited development of French firms in the consumer goods sector, on the other hand (pp. 31–2 above), has been related to the continuing dominance of its rural sector into the 1930s; the relative self-sufficiency of farming house-holds depressing mass demand for clothing and branded foodstuffs (Daviet, in Pohl, 1988; 73–87).

Considering the broader influence of what might be called 'consumer culture', Payne contrasts the 'ingrained preferences of British consumers for articles exhibiting "craftsmanship" and individual character' with the American 'willingness to accept a mass-produced standardised product' (1967; 524). Such tastes may have limited the scope for mass production in Britain (as well as France). Nevertheless, it is important to remember that Britain's markets were better integrated than elsewhere, partly as a function of her earlier industrialisation, and that per capita G.D.P. was the highest amongst the world's industrial nations until America pushed her into second place around 1899/1900. In those terms, Britain can be seen as further along the path towards developing a mass market for consumer goods than any other economy, and this helps account for the dominance of food and textile producers amongst her leading firms before 1939 (pp. 31–2 above).

The relationship between expanding markets and the growth of big business is by no means a simple one. In the American case, for example, Atack (1986) finds it difficult to correlate concentration with market-integrating transportation developments between the 1850s and 1870s. Instead, total demand and the number of firms in many areas of industry grew so rapidly that there was no clear trend in either direction. Nevertheless, it remains the case that for many industries such as branded, packaged foods and primary metals, large-scale manufacturing and vertical integration were only feasible where the market was able to absorb huge quantities of a standardised product.

Technological factors directly prompted vertical integration and the growth of firms to the extent that improved processes allowed increasing economies of scale. By utilising new, high-capacity machinery or furnaces, coupled with a careful rearrangement of successive processing stages so as to achieve smoother and speedier through-put, firms in many industries were able greatly to increase output volume whilst reducing unit costs. But it must be borne in mind that such scale economies only applied within single plants, and therefore do little to explain the growth of multi-plant firms (Penrose, 1959; *89–92*; Williamson, 1985; *273*). Similarly, it is important to acknowledge a distinction between internal and external economies of scale. While the former reflected the gains from high-volume production techniques within a plant, the latter represented the development of ancillary advantages, such as specialist commodity exchanges or components manufacturers, which benefitted all firms in an industry. Thus, while the British cotton textile industry expanded considerably between the 1750s and 1850s, this was achieved largely through the exploitation of external economies (Hannah, 1983; *9–10*). This, coupled with the limited scope for further internal scale economies after about the 1850s, meant that few really large firms developed in this sector, in Britain or elsewhere (see p. 17 above).

Potential economies of scale differed considerably between industries and in this context a useful distinction can be drawn between what Landes calls 'transforming' and 'assembling' processes (1969; *303–17*). With the former, such as oil refining, metallurgy or food processing, continuous flow techniques, and what Chandler calls 'economies of speed' (1977; *244*), were more readily obtained than in the latter, such as machine building or clothing manufacture. It is therefore not surprising that many of the classic examples of economies of scale are in the transforming industries. In steel making, for example, Andrew Carnegie opened an integrated plant at Pittsburgh in 1875 – the Edgar Thomson works – where careful planning to ensure smooth material flows, a huge scale of output and obsessive cost control enabled him to produce steel rails at around half the price which had prevailed until then. Within a year, the 'E.T.' was out-producing every other steel rail plant in the United States; Carnegie's former employer, the Pennsylvania Railroad, being assiduously cultivated as a major customer (Wall, 1970; *312–47*). Thermal economies encouraged vertical integration in iron and steel making, as in other transforming industries; considerable fuel savings being possible by keeping the metal molten as it moved from one processing stage to the next, although Lamoreaux questions the extent to which this happened in practice. She also comments that backward integration, in the case of the steel industry into iron ore mining, also helped control vital raw materials and, along with relentless cost-cutting strategies like those practised by Carnegie, provided powerful 'barriers to entry' by potential competitors (1985; *37–8, 144–7*).

In contrast to the gains from vertical integration in such fields as petroleum, steel and meat-packing in America during the 1870s and 1880s, similar economies came more slowly in the assembling industries since they required a more radical re-ordering of labour and machinery, as well as closer coordination of production flows. This helps explain the continuing fragmentation of enterprise in areas like clothing manufacture (Chandler, 1990; *22*). It also underlines the remarkable achievement of Henry Ford in pioneering an assembly line, mass-production process for such a complex product as the automobile. His Highland Park plant, opened in 1910 on a green-field site at Detroit, was designed from the outset to facilitate the flow of the new Model T through the assembly process. Rigorous attention to detail (partly influenced by new ideas on 'scientific management' articulated by men like Frederick W. Taylor) and ruthless abandonment of unsuitable techniques soon permitted a massive rise in output coupled with dramatic cost reductions. In 1909, before the assembly line method was introduced, just over 12,000 Model T Fords were sold, at around $950 each; by 1916 sales had risen to 577,000 while the basic price had fallen to $360. This achievement was partly a result of pronounced economies of scale and speed (the average time for assembling a chassis falling from 12.5 man-hours in June 1913, to 1.5 man-hours in January 1914), and partly because lower prices opened up a previously unimaginable mass market for cars (Nevins and Hill, 1954; *387–475*; Hounshell, 1984; *224–39*). Eventually, Henry Ford's autocratic personality and an inflexible product strategy drove his top executives to General Motors, which overtook him as leading vehicle producer by the late 1920s (Hounshell, 1984; *12–13, 261–4*; Chandler, 1990; *599*). Nevertheless, his success with the assembly line both symbolised a new era of mass production and pointed the way for similar developments in other industries.

As with so many other areas of manufacturing, the rather fragmented European motor industry tended to embrace 'Fordism' somewhat reluctantly before 1939 (Landes, 1969; *315, 440–51*), although there were exceptions, like Renault (p. 38 above). In general, greater American enthusiasm for mechanisation and capital-intensive techniques may be explicable in terms of relative labour scarcity, as suggested by Habakkuk (1962), in comparing American and British industry. However, Field (1987) argues that American big business was more effective in economising on capital, rather than labour. There is also a problem in reconciling a sharper trend towards capital-intensive technologies in many areas of German industry, compared with Britain, whilst industrial wages were generally lower in the former.

An inevitable consequence of the trend towards vertical integration and mass production was a rising ratio of fixed to total assets in the firms concerned, while improved coordination of production flows and resulting economies of speed allowed them to reduce inventories of raw materials and semi-finished goods. Both can be seen in the Du Pont balance sheets; plant and property exhibiting a long-term increase from 39 to 66 per cent of total assets between 1809 and 1951, while inventories fell from 24 to 11 per cent.[24] Rising fixed costs perplexed late-nineteenth-century manufacturers, inasmuch as they inhibited their ability to cut prices in the face of competitive pressures – just as they had done with railway companies (p. 15 above). Indeed, Lamoreaux explains the 1895–1904 merger wave in the United States primarily as an attempt 'to escape the severe price competition that developed during the depression of the nineties' by firms in capital-intensive, mass-production industries, which had expanded rapidly (and therefore increased their debt burden) on the eve of the 1893 panic (1985; *87*).

Technological factors influenced business concentration in other ways. Numerous writers, including Galbraith, have suggested that large corporations enjoyed a comparative advantage in funding increasingly expensive and time-consuming R&D programmes (1972; *23–39*), although this view has been questioned by Mowery (1983; *954–67*). From a different perspective, it is clear that product diversification strategies explain many cases of rapid corporate growth. The British textiles firm Courtaulds, for example, became a major multinational and saw its market capitalisation soar from $7.3 million in 1912 to $348 million in 1937, largely on the basis of its diversification from natural into artificial fibres (rayon) (Coleman, 1969; II: *20–42, 171–243*). R&D effort could also constitute a barrier to entry in an industry (Mueller, 1986; *108–18*). As the American photography pioneer George Eastman wrote in 1896, 'If we can get out improved goods every year nobody will be able to follow us and compete with us' (Chandler, 1977; *572*). It is equally clear that R&D effort, and consequent product diversification (see p. 33 above) could act as a new form of competition between firms otherwise appearing to enjoy oligopolistic control in an industry, a classic example being the pre-1939 German electrical goods sector (Landes, 1969; *353*).

Innovations in office technology, such as typewriters and telephones, helped increasingly large bureaucracies to function efficiently. The number of phones in use in the United States, for example, rose from 3000 in 1876 to 13 million by 1920, or one to eight inhabitants. In Britain, by way of contrast, there was only one to 48 inhabitants in 1920, perhaps confirming a view of British technological conservatism.[25] The coming of the 'skyscraper' (the first was built in Chicago in 1883) also facilitated the concentration of head office staff in city-centre sites.

A number of problems remain, in relating technology to big business. It is clear, for example, that some forms of technological innovation can actually promote the proliferation of small firms; a prime example being the development of flexible, low-cost electrical power, which benefitted many small-scale factories from the 1880s onwards (Prais, 1976; *52–3*). It is also evident that links between markets, technology and economies of scale are complex.

In particular, mass production needed assured mass markets and so, according to Chandler: 'Except in the production of primary metals, a manufacturing enterprise rarely became and remained large until it had built its own extensive marketing organisation' (1977; *364*). This was especially true with branded consumer goods – a good example arising from the introduction of the Bonsack cigarette making machine in Britain, by Wills, in 1884. With each machine capable of producing 300 cigarettes a minute, around 1890, the 15 then installed by Wills were more than capable of supplying total British demand. So, not only was Wills quickly propelled into a position where it dominated the growing cigarette market but it also had to devote increasing resources to marketing; including mass advertising and branding strategies, like the highly successful introduction of 'penny cigarettes' in 1888 (Alford, 1973; *143–225*). In other words, so high was the 'minimum efficient scale' of employing the Bonsack machine, that it was imperative to attract a steady flow of new customers. Intensive advertising and brand proliferation also offered potential advantages to market leaders, in acting as barriers to entry; areas of corporate activity which have attracted much attention in the recent literature, under the heading 'strategic behaviour' (Clarke and McGuinness, 1987; *12–14, 62–82*). There was similar pressure for forward integration where technologically complex goods required specialist marketing and after-sales support; examples including Singer (sewing machines) and McCormick (agricultural machinery) (Chandler, 1977; *302–12*).

A complex interplay of cause and effect between market growth and technological change makes it difficult to draw any simple conclusions about their relationship with one another, or with increasing business concentration. Not only did market integration stimulate cost-reducing manufacturing innovations, which fed back to further market growth, but employment and incomes generated in these industries further boosted mass demand. It is also necessary to recognise that all of these developments would have been of limited consequence but for major organisational innovation – in the structure and management of firms – and it is to this that we turn in the next chapter.

5
Markets, hierarchies and the managerial revolution

A predominant theme in recent analysis of business concentration has been the view that the visible hand of managerial coordination supersedes the invisible hand of the market mechanism, where it is possible to economise on a variety of costs involved in using the latter. There has also been considerable discussion of the ways in which the objectives of managerial firms differ from those of entrepreneurial firms (as defined on p. 8 above), and how these differences influence corporate growth.

Transaction costs, the market and the firm

In a theorem which continues to pervade many areas of economic theory and policy, Adam Smith argued that competitive markets, with a multitude of small producers basing business decisions on price signals, provide the most effective and impartial mechanism for ordering economic transactions within society (Mueller, 1986; *261*). This may have been a fair approximation of reality in 1776, or even as late as the 1840s (pp. 54–5 above). By the 1930s, however, a growing number of scholars, such as Berle and Means (1932; *345–6*), were expressing reservations about Smith's view of the world. Particularly significant was Ronald Coase's perception that firms and markets represent alternative methods of organising production (1937). Within a competitive market, for example, steel-makers would arrange their ore and fuel supplies in terms of relative prices set by independent mining companies; whilst a vertically-integrated firm would organise such raw material flows in response to orders transmitted from one branch of management to another. Observing the wide variety of organisational modes in the business world in the 1930s – from giant, hierarchical corporations to a host of small firms – Coase was prompted to ask 'why coordination is the work of the price mechanism in one case and of the entrepreneur in another' (1937; *389*).

His answer – one which was to profoundly influence later developments in the theory of the firm – was that there were costs associated with using the price system, such as those associated with discovering relevant prices and in arranging contracts for each market transaction. At the same time, Coase recognised that there were costs involved in organising transactions within firms, particularly in countering bureaucratic inefficiency. Consequently, he suggested that 'a firm will tend to expand until the costs of organising an extra transaction within the firm become equal to the costs of carrying out the same transaction by means of an exchange on the open market or the costs of organising in another firm' (1937; *395*). Given the diversity of these 'transaction costs' between different economic activities, it also seemed relatively easy explaining why exchange internalisation, and corporate expansion, varied so considerably. Although he was primarily concerned with explaining the existence of firms in general, as 'islands of conscious power in [an] ocean of unconscious co-operation' (1937; *388*), his theorem has proved, by extension, a powerful tool of analysis of the growth of big business.

Rather surprisingly, Coase's transaction costs approach languished in virtual obscurity until the 1970s, when Oliver Williamson extended and refined the theorem, primarily in his book *Market and Hierarchies* (1975). A key reason for this neglect, according to Williamson, was that the Coase theorem was too weakly specified to enable systematic analysis of the distribution of transactions between firms and markets (1975; *3–4*); apart from which, he argues, 'the study of institutional economics reached a nadir in the immediate postwar period' (1985; *15–16*).

Williamson's ideas are complex, but merit discussing at some length; particularly since they have played a major role in re-orientating study of big business from traditional concerns, such as monopoly-seeking behaviour and technological imperatives, towards seeing large-scale corporation as an efficiency instrument, internalising functions otherwise performed by the price system.

Like Coase, he argues that the growth of firms can largely be explained in terms of attempts to economise on transaction costs. However, he goes further by specifying those costs in contractual terms; as 'the *ex ante* costs of negotiating and writing, as well as the *ex post* costs of executing, policing, and, when disputes arise, remedying the (explicit or implicit) contract that joins . . .' technologically separable economic activities (1986; *139*). He also suggests that transaction costs can only be examined systematically in relation to three factors: bounded rationality, opportunism and asset specificity (1985; *30–67*).

Bounded rationality, a behavioural concept developed by Herbert Simon in the 1950s, starts with the assumption that 'economic actors' have limited capacity for absorbing and utilising information. So, while they may aim to make rational decisions, the virtual impossibility of comprehending every possible outcome of a situation, and of obtaining every relevant fact, means they invariably make less than fully rational decisions (Williamson, 1975; *2–10, 21–5*). Merchants trading in Smithian competitive markets, for example, would find it prohibitively costly to monitor every market signal or to contract for every contingency; although, in such conditions, they would not normally need to do so. Opportunism refers to various forms of guileful behaviour, such as misrepresenting the quality of goods; it only being necessary for some people to act this way to result in general uncertainty about who is acting honestly in a market (Clarke and McGuinness, 1987; *44–5*). Asset specificity reflects the extent to which resources are dedicated to particular uses, and how much their value will be diminished if used in alternative ways. Williamson distinguishes at least three major types: physical asset specificity, where particular skills are required in a work-force; and site specificity, where successive production stages are located near each other in order to economise on inventory and transportation costs (1986; *141–2*). Thus, a blast-furnace has little value outside the primary metals sector, research chemists or machine-tool operators are of little use in other employment (short of costly retraining), and a factory built near one supplier cannot readily be moved if another supplier is subsequently preferred. With high levels of asset specificity, buyers and sellers become 'locked into' one another, as their level of transaction-specific investment induces an aversion to contract termination, even if unforeseen circumstances arise or they suspect they are subject to opportunism by the other party.

Williamson concludes that bounded rationality combined with opportunism, in the absence of asset specificity, will not generally stimulate internalisation, since the parties to an exchange will have no hesitation in arranging alternative contracts. However, the simultaneous existence of all three factors leads to high transaction costs in market-based exchange and strong incentives to internalise (1985; *33–4*). And, he continues, it is this recognition which enables us to make effective use of the Coase theorem and explain why internalisation and the development of big business have displayed such variability. Rather like the desire for monopoly power, bounded rationality and opportunism can be assumed to have always existed, in some form, in market-exchange environments. However, asset specificity would have increased considerably with the growth of railways and public utilities, followed by capital-intensive, mass-production manufacturing, in the century before World War II. In this context, Williamson also emphasises the role of 'transaction frequency', in making internalisation preferable to market exchange (1986; *141–3*). Where particular transactions (flows of goods) are standardised and frequently recurring, internalisation costs (setting up managerial hierarchies) will be more readily recovered, and the transactional savings over market exchange correspondingly larger. This accords with Chandler's emphasis on 'economies of speed' and the view that internalisation advantages, and particularly forward integration into marketing, came more readily in 'transforming' processes (see pp. 57–8 above).

Moving transactions from markets to firms is seen as economising on bounded rationality and opportunism in a number of ways. According to Williamson, it 'permits adaptations to uncertainty to be accomplished by administrative processes in a sequential fashion'; 'the parties to an internal exchange are less able to appropriate subgroup gains at the expense of the overall organization'; 'internal organizations can be more effectively audited'; and 'when differences do arise, internal organization realizes an advantage over market mediated exchange in dispute settling respects' (1975; *9, 29*). Opportunism and uncertainty in labour markets might also encourage internalisation; seen, in the nineteenth century, in a shift from the weakly supervised putting-out system to the more tightly controlled environment of factory employment (Braverman, 1974; *60–3*).

In emphasising transaction costs explanations in the growth of firms, Williamson does not entirely dismiss other factors, such as strategic behaviour (1975; *2, 20*) or technological imperatives. However, he argues that even classic exemplars of the latter, like vertically-integrated steel firms, can be better understood in transactional terms, on the basis that 'steady state thermal economies can always be realised by placing autonomous blast furnaces and rolling mills alongside one another, whatever the ownership structure' (1985; *125*). It would be the contractual difficulties which would make such arrangements less attractive than common ownership. Moreover, unlike economies of scale, transaction cost arguments do help explain the growth of multi-plant firms (see p. 57 above). Against this, some of the world's largest firms of the pre-1939 era, copper producers like Anaconda and Kennecott, arguably expanded more as a result of technological, rather than transactional, pressures (Schmitz, 1986). Additionally, Chandler emphasises that internalisation brought potential gains, not only in terms of lower transaction costs, but also by permitting closer coordination between supply and demand. This led to improved control of raw materials and higher volume throughput; the latter generating cash flows which could dramatically reduce the unit cost of fixed and working capital (1977; *286*).

The transaction costs theorem has greatly influenced recent theoretical work on corporate growth, particularly in such areas as multinational enterprise (Caves, 1982; *16–18*). On the other hand, its role in historical studies of big business has been a rather uneasy one. Whilst many recent works, such as Chandler (1977), explicitly acknowledge the Coase-Williamson schema, there remains some hesitancy in its application. Hannah, for example, only specifically talks about transaction costs in the context of financial markets (1983; *62–3, 66*). Where recent business histories have been written with an eye to the theoretical literature, it is not difficult to detect transactional motives in specific episodes of corporate expansion. Ferrier, for example, describes a determination 'to build up an absolutely self-contained organization' at Anglo-Persian Oil; realised through a vigorous strategy of forward integration in the post World War I era (1982; *160, 461–537)*. Even amongst an older generation of studies, it is possible to impute analogous motives. William Lever's backward integration into raw materials, between 1895 and 1912, has been discussed in terms of his desire for 'independence of the market' (Wilson, 1954; I: *183–4)*. Similarly, following a visit to the United States in 1903, Carl Duisberg, one of the founders of I. G. Farben, advocated a merger of leading German chemical producers, on the basis that one of the benefits of 'common management must always be the largest possible reduction in the costs of production, administration and sale . . .' (Maschke, 1969; *243)*. Nevertheless, many business historians remain sceptical about the practical value of such theoretical constructs (see pp. 80–1 below).

Critiques of Williamson's markets and hierarchies approach have come from a number of directions. Fitzroy and Mueller (in Mueller, 1986; *51–77)* contend that he says too little about the distributional implications, as opposed to efficiency gains, from the expansion of hierarchies. Thus, in allocating profits between managers and stockholders, or managers and labour, the former might appropriate considerable gains for themselves, as managerial perks or pay-rises. In the context of multinational enterprise, it has been suggested that no general theory, like transaction costs, can mirror the complexity of foreign direct investment; instead a more flexible, adaptive approach is required (Dunning, 1988; *11–12*; Casson, in Clarke and McGuinness, 1987; *139–41)*. Nicholas has also argued that Williamson's model is too static, making no allowance for evolving modes of internalisation (in Hertner and Jones, 1986; *64–79)*. Instead, it should be recognised that firms, like Lever Brothers, often opened their own foreign subsidiaries after they had experienced shortcomings in dealing through independent agencies. It might also be argued that the transactional theorem is weakened by a failure to locate it within a comparative socio-cultural framework. Williamson hints at such a possibility when he suggests that 'markets often work better than a "legalistic" analysis would suggest because of institutional adaptations by businessmen' (1975; *106)*. This would tie in with the view that, in contrast with the impersonal commercial regime of the United States (pp. 52–3 above), European businessmen (particularly in Britain and France) evolved more robust 'personal' market exchange institutions; where intimacy and trust went further towards countering bounded rationality and opportunism.

It is clear that the transaction costs theorem is extremely difficult to test empirically, particularly in a historical context. This, in part, has led scholars like Chandler (1977; 1990) and Hannah (1983) to stress a broader conjunction of transactional, technological and institutional factors in the rise of big business. Typical of recent research in this mould, is Langlois and Robertson's (1989) analysis of vertical integration in the pre-1939 American automobile industry, which argues that while no single theory is entirely sufficient, a transaction costs approach offers the most convincing general explanation.

Managerial hierarchies, organization building and the limits to firms

With the movement of increasing volumes of transactions from markets to firms, alternative allocative and signalling mechanisms had to evolve, to replace the 'invisible hand' of the price system. The development of such organisational structures and monitoring procedures had, in turn, two major implications for the continuing growth of business corporations. First, in the hierarchies which evolved, corporate policy was increasingly dictated either by a new class of salaried managers or, perhaps more realistically, as a result of compromises between the different interest groups in a firm – management, stockholders and labour – but with the former generally in a dominant position. Secondly, the difficulty of establishing and refining these bureaucratic structures meant that, in weighing up the relative cost of markets and hierarchies as governance structures, certain limits to the growth of firms became apparent; helping answer Coase's query: 'Why is not all production carried on by one big firm?' (1937; 394).

The evolution of managerial hierarchies and monitoring procedures followed many paths from the railway era onwards (pp. 11–15, 33–41 above), but two key ingredients permitting the efficient operation of ever larger bureaucracies were increasing managerial professionalism and improved cost accounting, as well as other forms of statistical monitoring, within firms. The salaried manager

– what Chandler has called 'a new subspecies of economic man' (1977; *484*) – made his first, widespread appearance in the railway companies of the 1850s and 1860s. By the late nineteenth century, management training was becoming more formalised, at least in the United States, with the growth of professional societies and the establishment of institutions like the Wharton Business School (1881) and the Harvard Business School (1908). Growing demand for salaried managers was also evident; in the United States their numbers rising from 352,000 in 1900 to 1.35 million in 1930 (Lazonick, in Kobayashi and Morikawa, 1986; *110*). At the level of the individual organisation, administrative staff at the German firm Siemens rose from nine to 29 per cent of all employees between 1865 and 1912; by which time the Berlin headquarters had nearly three thousand office workers (Kocka, 1971; *148–50*). Modern cost accounting techniques, likewise, had their origins in the railways of the 1850s and 1860s, but were greatly refined by Pierre S. du Pont and the managerial team at Du Pont, in the period 1903–10. According to Chandler, their development of sophisticated accounting and statistical controls, utilising detailed data on such things as productivity and sales, allowed them to systematically evaluate managerial performance, profitability and market conditions, even within an increasingly large and diverse organisation; and, in turn, this became a widely-imitated model for many other businesses (1977; *443–8*).

Organisation building – refining hierarchies and procedures, as well as recruiting and training new managers – is widely regarded as having been the greatest challenge facing top management during the past century (Chandler, 1962; *36–41*). Expanding firms faced similar problems in this respect, but followed a wide variety of routes to their solution. At one extreme, Rockefeller's Standard Oil Trust of 1882 passed through a period of rather confused managerial organisation before 1911, with a clearly defined hierarchy and lines of communication between its diverse parts only emerging in piecemeal fashion (Hidy and Hidy, 1955; *112–331*). In sharp contrast, Du Pont moved purposefully through a series of organisational changes between 1903 and 1921, which equipped it to expand into the world's largest and most innovative chemicals firm of the interwar period and beyond (Chandler, 1962; *52–113*; Hounshell and Smith, 1988).

The diversity of ways in which firms progressed towards these new organisational structures is evident in the extent to which perceptions about managerial limits to the growth of firms continued into the interwar period. Such views had a long history; Adam Smith, echoing a belief widespread in the late eighteenth century, argued that salaried managers would not exercise the same diligence in overseeing a company's affairs, as would the owners. Therefore, firms should cease to expand beyond the point where undue delegation of responsibility to non-family managers became necessary; unless operations were capable of being reduced to a relatively simple routine, as in banking, which did witness an earlier development of professional management than manufacturing (Pollard, 1965; *10–24*). Whilst the managerial innovations of the pre World War I era helped many American and European firms break free of these long-standing constraints, there remained considerable pessimism, especially in Britain, about the ability to administer very large companies; despite the much-vaunted advantages of 'rationalization' during the 1920s (Hannah, 1983; *70–89*). Even in a progressive firm like Courtaulds, plans to absorb all other British rayon producers were dropped in 1937; primarily due to management's belief that weaknesses in the company's organisation would make such an amalgamation 'complicated and necessarily highly centralized' and that 'large scale policy and finance are beyond the scope of most of us' (Coleman, 1969; II: *237–8*).

The growing importance of professional management and the divorce of ownership and control, in what has been dubbed the 'managerial revolution', has prompted scholars to re-evaluate traditional economic theory, which implied that firms functioned in terms of simplistic profit-maximising motives. The possibility that the objectives of managers and owners (stockholders) might differ, has long been recognised (Hilferding, 1910; *126*). More recently, a number of writers have suggested, in what can be labelled 'managerial theories' of the firm, that salaried executives might seek to maximise something other than profits: Baumol arguing in terms of sales maximisation, Marris in terms of corporate growth, and Williamson in relation to managerial prestige and perks (Lee, 1990; *19*). Although none of these is incompatible with long-run profit maximisation, managers might sacrifice profits (dividends) in the shorter run, in order to achieve one or more of the other goals, which would, in turn, enhance their career security and professional status. Other writers, particularly Cyert and March, developed what can be called 'behavioural theories' of the firm; arguing that such organisations function as arenas within which the conflicting interests of different groups – managers, stockholders and labour (or sub-groups within these categories) – can be reconciled. Firms thus become satisficing organisations, which, rather than maximising any particular function, optimalise conflicting goals (Lee, 1990; *20*).

Whilst behavioural theories of the firm seem particularly difficult to operationalise within a historical context, aspects of the managerial theories have been strongly paralleled in Chandler's work. Amongst other things, he suggests that, once formed, managerial hierarchies became sources of 'permanence, power and continued growth'. Managerial enterprise thus took on (in Werner Sombart's terms) 'a life of its own', unlike family firms which frequently died with their owners (1977; *8*). Consequently, the size, power and prestige of such corporations would generally have been reinforced by the status-seeking activities of succeeding generations of managers; although, as noted below, managerial torpor might counter this trend at any stage.

Inasmuch as Chandler's ideas concerning the rise of managerial capitalism have profoundly influenced the discipline of business history since the early 1960s, it is important to recognise four particular areas of potential difficulty in his approach. First, he has been criticised for saying virtually nothing about the labour dimension of corporate growth and management (Williamson, in Chandler and Daems, 1980; *196*). In contrast, Braverman (1974) has argued that an understanding of labour is central to analysis of big business; highlighting, in particular, the potential for worker alienation within large-scale bureaucracies, with consequent implications for labour diseconomies of scale. In similar vein, Hounshell notes that Ford experienced very high staff turnover when establishing his assembly-line system around 1910–15, and so had to offer unusually high wages to retain employees within an increasingly routinised work environment (1984; *11*). Secondly, there is no consideration of alternative institutional modes of corporate control, particularly in his treatment of the British business system (Chandler, 1990; *235–392*). Other writers have examined the apparently slow development of British big business, especially before 1914, and have suggested that informal networks of control, via interlocking directorships (Scott and Griff, 1984) and informally-constituted investment groups (Chapman, 1985), represented alternative forms of business concentration, more favoured within the non-bureaucratic British business tradition. A similar pattern is implied in the investment groupings within French business before the 1950s (Houssiaux, 1958; *236–41*). Against this, it is difficult to determine the practical significance of such networks and, in any case, similar structures were apparent in areas of American and German business, especially before about 1918 (see pp. 45–6 above). Thirdly, in common with many other leading studies, like Hannah (1983), Chandler says little about the service sector (apart from railways), despite its palpable importance in all maturing capitalist economies (Wardley, 1991). Banks, for example, were amongst the most heavily capitalised concerns in America and Europe in the pre-1939 era (Born, 1983; *66–99, 231– 51*), and yet they are generally only considered in terms of their role as providers of industrial capital. Finally, from the perspective of the de-merger wave of the 1980s, it is worthwhile questioning both Chandler's general lack of emphasis on purely financial considerations in corporate regroupings (1977; *373–4*), and the extent to which the 'modern corporation' represents, in any sense, the final outcome of a long-term process of organisational evolution.

In broader terms, consideration of the advantages of internalisation should not obscure the continuing importance of markets: in regulating final demand for the products of integrated firms, in mediating relations between large corporations, or as reflected in the remarkable vitality of small firms in many areas of economic activity. Indeed, market-exchange remained more attractive in many areas of activity, such as clothing manufacture, for a variety of technological and organisational reasons (p. 58 above). This is underlined by the fact that two-thirds of all American corporations reported net earnings of less than $5,000 in 1927 (Berle and Means, 1932; *18*).

A useful starting point, in these terms, is Williamson's suggestion that 'transactions will be organised by markets unless market exchange gives rise to serious transaction costs' (1986; *143*). This is because, as Coase recognised, the costs of using market mechanisms have to be weighed against the potentially equally serious costs arising from internalisation: the transaction costs within firms (1937; *394–6*). Penrose highlights the internalisation costs associated with improving the quality of managerial services: training new managers often diverting resources from existing management (1959; *258–9*). Williamson talks of the potential costs of bureaucracy; suggesting that a corporate culture may emerge which inhibits organisational innovation (1985; *148–53*). Moreover, such torpor may not easily be rectified, as stockholders' attempts to displace incumbent managers are not always easy (Williamson, 1975; *128*). This was evident in the difficulty within which J. D. Rockefeller unseated the chairman of Standard Oil (Indiana) in 1929, despite owning 15 per cent of the voting stock (Galbraith, 1967; *92–3*).

Generalised limits to the growth of firms were identified by Coase; when the complexity of operations reached such a state that there were 'decreasing returns to the entrepreneurial function', with managers making sub-optimal use of factors, as they lost command of information flows and allocative mechanisms (1937; *394–5*). To a certain extent, these managerial limitations could be overcome by organisational adaptations; a classic example being the shift from U-form to M-form hierarchies by firms like Du Pont (p. 35 above). Williamson notes that one of the problems of the U-form was that 'managers identified with functional interests and hence were more given to subgroup pursuit', while top managers found it difficult disengaging themselves from competing departmental claims (1986; *157*). Also, 'bounded rationality gives rise to finite spans of control', especially where 'increasing firm size leads to taller hierarchies' as in centralised (U-form) structures (1975; *126–7*). So, in order to overcome creeping managerial paralysis, and to enable the hierarchy to adequately mimic the market as an allocative governance structure, a disinterested top layer of management had to be created. Freed from mundane operational decision-making, they could concentrate on long-term strategy as well as arbitrating between conflicting divisional interests. Such thinking is apparent in the move towards an M-form hierarchy undertaken by I.C.I. in 1930–1, when it was decided that top directors should be freed from 'some of the detailed duties', 'so that they could become advisers on major matters of policy' (Reader, 1975; *138–44*).

In sum, bearing in mind the shortcomings of any single-theory approach and the difficulty involved in applying such a framework within the historical context, Williamson convincingly suggests that 'the strongest argument favouring transaction cost economizing . . . is that this is the only hypothesis that is able to provide a discriminating rationale for the succession of organizational innovations that have occurred over the past 150 years and out of which the modern corporation has emerged' (1986; *163*).

6
The impact of big business

If debate concerning the nature and origins of big business has been protracted and wide-ranging, so also has analysis of its impact on social and political institutions, as well as its implications for economic growth and efficiency. Nevertheless, the key aspects of this discussion can be summarised in fairly brief terms.

Reactions: politics and regulation

Although anxiety about monopoly power predates the nineteenth century (see pp. 43–4 above), from around the 1860s the expansion of big business began to prompt new concerns. Joining traditional apprehensions about predacious associations of individual entrepreneurs, were vaguer fears about remote and impersonal business bureaucracies. However, such responses varied considerably in space and time. In Europe, apart from the writings of intellectuals like Macrosty (1907) and Hilferding (1910), there appears to have been relatively little ongoing antagonism towards cartels or combines. There could be specific episodes of heightened public unease, such as the British 'Soap Trust' affair of 1906, when leading manufacturers, including William Lever, had to abandon large-scale merger plans following concerted attacks in the popular press (Wilson, 1954; I: *69–88*). However, in general terms, such anti-business sentiment as existed, particularly in France and Britain, was arguably part of a broader 'landed-aristocratic' ethos (see pp. 50–1 above), and led to no consistent pressure for anti-monopoly legislation before the 1950s. In America, in sharp contrast, a widespread mood of antagonism towards big business emerged during the railroad era of the 1860s and 1870s, attained particular intensity during the economic downturn of the mid 1890s and the subsequent merger wave, before re-emerging in a less virulent form during the slump of the 1930s (Galambos, 1975). This mood helped propel the United States towards enacting the world's only systematic anti-monopoly legislation in the century before 1939 (McGraw, 1984), although other factors, such as the intervention of businessmen, may have been influential in shaping antitrust policy (see p. 49 above).

The apparent paradox of America being both the birth-place of modern managerial capitalism as well as home for such vigorous anti-corporativist sentiment, has provoked a considerable amount of study. Keller argues that the unparalleled rapidity with which American society was confronted by corporate capitalism, coupled with its lack of European-style traditions of feudalism or state bureaucracy, helps explain the strength of anti-big business feeling (in Chandler and Daems, 1980; 166). It has also been suggested that populist anti-business rhetoric was fuelled by apprehension about the decline of a society populated by small-scale merchants and farmers – Thomas Jefferson's comforting vision of agrarian-individualism – in the face of advancing urbanisation and bureau-cratisation (Galambos, 1975; 15–20). This fostering of what Richard Hofstadter termed 'the Agrarian Myth',[26] may have been one manifestation of a wider disquiet about rapid change in an industrialising society, but it was not unique to the United States. German National Socialist anti-business rhetoric in the 1920s and early 1930s was also founded to a considerable extent on anti-urban, agrarian-idealising notions (Turner, 1985; 67–75), while the Franco-British 'landed-aristocratic' ethos may have been a milder variant of the same theme.

A particular problem arises in distinguishing specific anxieties about big business from wider fears of rapid industrialisation and attendant challenges to antecedent social structures. Unfortu-nately, few studies have attempted to gauge popular perceptions of big business in the pre-1939 period, apart from the statistical work of Louis Galambos. His analysis of changing attitudes amongst various American social groupings suggests that there was a long term trend towards measured acceptance of the new corporate world (1975; 253–68). This accords with a broader historiographical tradition which regards the general thrust of the American populist and progressive movements of the 1890s and early 1900s, as well as antitrust policy with all its inconsistencies, as a 'search for order' – a nation groping towards an accommodation with novel concepts of social and business organisation.[27]

Changing perceptions of big business amongst a specific group, namely historians, also merit attention. Until the work of scholars like Alfred Chandler and Gabriel Kolko in the 1960s, American writing in particular seemed trapped in a rather polarised approach to the topic, and one which arguably over-emphasised the role of individual businessmen in the growth of large-scale enterprise. On the one hand there was the so-called 'robber baron' school, epitomised by writers like Ida Tarbell (1904). Such critics, dubbed 'muckrakers' by Theodore Roosevelt, provided useful ammunition for the progressive cause. In contrast, scholars like Allan Nevins (1940) portrayed such men as J. D. Rockefeller as 'industrial statesmen', whose achievements in creating new industries outweighed their occasional lapses of business propriety. The latter approach, though long unfashionable, can now be seen as having made a significant intellectual contribution to the gradual acceptance of corporate capitalism.

Effects: economic growth and welfare

The welfare implications of big business have been explored in a variety of directions, including the role of multinational enterprise in less developed countries (Baran and Sweezy, 1966; *192–201*; Caves, 1982; *252–78*) and the position of labour within the large corporation (Marglin, 1974; Braverman, 1974). However, a prime concern for many scholars has been to question the efficiency gains from increasing business concentration, both at the level of the individual firm and of national economies. The latter approach is particularly relevant to an argument that lacklustre British and French economic growth between the 1870s and 1950s, compared with the United States, resulted in significant measure from a relative failure to embrace the 'visible hand' of managerial capitalism. Such arguments are predicated on the assumption (discussed in Chapters 4 and 5) that large-scale, managerial firms enjoy certain advantages over regimes of small firms competing within the market place or federations of firms tied by agreement.

In these terms, the team of scholars assembled by Elbaum and Lazonick (1986) argues that the British economy was handicapped by a fragmented, over-competitive industrial system during most of the century before the 1960s. Using Chandler's vision of the achievements of the American business system as a yardstick, they find that key British industries, such as cotton textiles, steel and automobiles, lacked the managerial skills, the commitment to R&D and the ability to regulate the work environment which might have contributed to a more competitive and dynamic economy. Chandler has confirmed this damning interpretation, stating that, in Britain 'the economic costs of the commitment to personal management were high . . . By World War I the industrial output of the United States and Germany was outpacing that of Britain' (1990; *294*). In similar vein, Landes concluded that French economic performance for more than a century before 1950, was handicapped by the overwhelming dominance of small family enterprises '. . . with a firm distaste for the new and unknown' (1949; *48*).

Such interpretations are open to criticism at a number of levels. First, aggregate economic growth indicators only offer partial support for this approach. In the crucial 1870–1913 period, while the American growth rate was double Britain's (2.0 per cent per annum compared with 1.0 per cent), France, for all its fragmented, 'conservative' industrial structure, enjoyed a rate not significantly different from that in Germany (1.5 and 1.6 per cent respectively).[28] Secondly, the applicability of American yardsticks in the European context has already been questioned (pp. 36–7 above). This seems especially true in the French case, where recent scholarship has not only convincingly attacked traditional, pessimistic views of economic performance, but has suggested that the regime of small firms was a logical response to prevailing domestic conditions (Lévy-Leboyer, in Carter, Foster and Moody, 1976). Nye also criticises the Landes (1949) interpretation, arguing that a number of key industries exhibited constant returns to scale over a wide range of output, and so it is unlikely France would have gained much from having larger firms. He also reminds us that the incidence of small family firms was similar in France and Germany at the end of the nineteenth century (1987; *667*). Such doubts with the Chandler-Landes schema extend to Britain, where Hannah points to the paradox that despite apparently higher levels of business concentration than America or Germany by the 1960s, aggregate British economic performance still left much to be desired (1983; *162–3*). Thirdly, most studies critical of British and French business structures studiously ignore the service sector, despite its increasing significance in both economies (see p. 72 above).

Finally, there is a considerable degree of uncertainty, at a theoretical level, about the macroeconomic efficiency gains from increasing business concentration. As Marris and Mueller have argued 'there is no obvious connection, either way, between the prevalence of giant corporations and economic performance' (in Mueller, 1986; 262). This partly reflects long-standing deficiencies in the theory of the firm (as discussed in chapter 5). It should also warn us of the temporal and cultural limitations of the 'visible hand' paradigm, particularly in the circumstances of pre-1939 Britain or France, when the invisible hand of market forces arguably offered a more effective mechanism for coordinating economic transactions (Hannah, in Chandler and Daems, 1980; *63–5*).

7

Conclusions: history and theory

A complex interplay of factors appears to have shaped the growth of big business in America and Europe since the mid nineteenth century. Inevitably, many of the conclusions reached in this study are rather tentative; reflecting weaknesses in theory as well as gaps in the empirical record. Nevertheless, it is clear that recent scholarship tends towards the view that transaction cost explanations offer the most promising framework for approaching the general rise of the modern business corporation (Williamson, 1985; *387–8*). At the same time, variations in the evolution of big business are perhaps best explained in terms of 'differences in the technologies of production and distribution and differences in the sizes and locations of markets' (Chandler, 1990; *18*). Other factors, such as capital markets or socio-cultural values, may have had the capacity to modify these more powerful influences, as in pre-1914 Britain, but in themselves appear to have had little enduring effect on the growth of corporate capitalism.

It is important to recognise that a number of difficulties stand in the way of synthesising the profusion of contributions to this area of study. A prime concern – part of a wider methodological issue – is the long-standing tension between historians' and economists' approaches to deriving generalisations about the growth of big business. On the one hand, an economist like Edith Penrose can argue that the historian's habit of relying upon an accumulation of consistent examples represents a flawed proof of a case 'unless the examples are presented in sufficiently large numbers and selected in such a way that they constitute a representative sample' (1959; *3*). Her related criticism about a dearth of empirical evidence on the growth of firms has been remedied to a large extent since the

1950s, although it seems that the work of business historians continues to be biased towards the 'success stories' of corporate enterprise. On the other hand, historians can express scepticism about the practical value of concepts like transaction costs; asking if this is another of Clapham's celebrated 'empty boxes' of economic theory (Coleman, 1987; *152*). It is possible that the seeming inapplicability of this particular concept to many published company histories arises from the failure of their writers to ask the right questions of their material. However, the fragmented nature of the theory of the firm, coupled with a widely-acknowledged inability of neo-classical economics to explain corporate growth (Mueller, 1986; *262–4*), means that it is easy to conclude that any body of theory will fail to mirror the historical complexity of business evolution. This is particularly apparent in those cases when business consolidation arose in response to specific events; an example being the formation of Imperial Tobacco in 1901, following a hostile move into the British market by the American Tobacco Company (Alford, 1973; *251–64*).

Existing theory also has a problem dealing with the role of individual entrepreneurship. Historians will typically ask how much the growth of particular firms can be ascribed to the initiative or personality of specific business leaders, and what qualities differentiated these individuals in their successes and failures? Emphasising the crucial role of William Lever in the growth of Unilever, Charles Wilson argues:

There is a view of economic history which regards the capitalist only as a cork bobbing on the economic tide. To regard a phenomenon such as the Lever business merely as an inevitable result of the tendency towards large-scale organisation and the destruction of competition would be to court ridicule. Without Lever there would have been no Lever Brothers, and the whole structure of a national industry . . . might have worn a very different aspect. (1954; I: *291*)

It is true that distrust of 'entrepreneurial' explanations of corporate growth is shared by some historians, most notably Alfred Chandler (1977; *373*). To a certain extent, this may represent continuing dissatisfaction with the 'robber baron' and 'industrial statesmen' schools of thought (see p. 77 above). However, it is equally clear that the growth of no firm is divorced from the historically dominant culture of its owners or upper and middle managers, and it is in this realm that the historian's approach is perhaps more flexible than that afforded by organisational or economic theory.

Another acute methodological problem arises, as in many other areas of economic history, from the difficulty in disengaging cause and effect when analysing the growth of big business. Reference has already been made (in Chapter 4) to this difficulty in relation to capital markets and socio-cultural value systems. Such multi-directional causality is hardly surprising, given the complex inter-action between factors like market expansion, organisational and technological innovation, and the potential for economies of scale (p. 61 above). However, it does suggest that analysis of changing industrial structures should be approached with due caution and without emphasising individual factors in isolation.

Whatever difficulties arise in reconciling various approaches to the historical growth of big business, there is widespread agree-ment that the agenda for future research should include many more empirical studies of individual firms and industries, but that these must, as far as possible, be informed by questions suggested by evolving theory in such diverse fields as multinational enter-prise, technological innovation and organisational behaviour. In this way, we may move towards a better understanding of the forces that have shaped the giant enterprises which dominate the late twentieth century world economy, as well as the factors which continue to place limits on their power.

Notes

1. Although the absolute scale of business enterprise has increased rapidly since World War II, the growth paths of many firms which continue to dominate global markets were firmly established before 1939. A prime example is General Motors (GM) of the USA, which was ranked first amongst world manufacturing firms in 1937 (by market value of issued stock) as well as in 1987 (measured by sales revenue). As an absolute measure of GM's expansion since its early years, its gross sales revenue (in 1987 prices) was $1.23 billion in 1918, $11.1 billion in 1937 and $101.8 billion in 1987 (*Moody's Manual* 1939, *Times 1000 1988–89*). More generally, 21 of the top 50 American and European non-state sector industrials of 1987 (*Times 1000 1988–89*), including the first five, were survivors from the list of 1937 (Table 2, pp. 24–5).

   The only other significant development of large-scale, multi-unit business enterprise before 1939, comparable with that in the United States and western Europe, occurred in Japan. Recent research indicates that the early twentieth-century Japanese economy was developing familiar aspects of industrial concentration; including widespread cartelisation, vertical integration and modern managerial practices. However, in other respects, the very distinctive character of Japanese society influenced divergences from the American and European patterns of corporate growth; in particular, the development of the powerful *zaibatsu* industrial-commercial-financial combines (literally translating as 'money cliques'). By the 1920s, the leading *zaibatsu*, including Mitsui, Mitsubishi and Sumitomo, controlled extensive networks of extractive, manufacturing and transportation enterprises, each centred on a financial core which typified this form of business organisation (Morikawa, in Pohl, 1988; *49–66*). What particularly differentiated these pre-1939 Japanese business organisations from western big business, was the extent to which they had already become diversified conglomerates, engaging in a wide range of unrelated activities. Such forms only emerged in western business during the 1960s and 1970s, an example being the Anglo-American conglomerate Hanson Plc (Williamson, 1986; *154–8*; Clarke and McGuinness, 1987; *107–9*).

The development of Japanese big business is not specifically discussed in this study, partly for reasons of brevity and partly due to the distinctive cultural factors which set the growth of organisations like Mitsui and Mitsubishi quite apart from that of large-scale western firms. Additionally, even the largest Japanese firms were not particularly big, by western standards, before World War II. Nippon Steel, the largest individual Japanese industrial firm in 1935, had capital assets equivalent to around $136 million, which would have placed it well outside the world's top 50 firms (Table 2, pp. 24–5); Y. Suzuki, *Japanese Management Structures, 1920–80* (London, 1991); *334*. Taking the leading *zaibatsu* conglomerates as a whole suggests a somewhat higher level of importance: the total issued capital of the Mitsui combine (including subsidiary interests) was equivalent to around $330 million in 1937, while that of the Mitsubishi group was $237 million; N. S. Smith, 'Japan's Business Families' *Economist*, June 18, 1938; *655*.

2. Leslie Hannah, for example, in reviewing *Scale and Scope*, expresses a marked degree of reservation about the general applicability of many aspects of Chandler's paradigm, when discussed in terms of British and German experience: 'Scale and Scope: Towards a European Visible Hand?' *Business History*, XXXIII (1991); *298–306*.

3. Fixed capital represents investment in buildings and equipment; working capital equals the value of stocks of raw materials, part-processed and finished goods, as well as trade debts (goods or services sold but not yet paid for). A key distinction between the two is that a firm has the option of reducing the cost of financing its working capital, as well as its labour bill, by curtailing production during a depression, whereas the burden of fixed costs remains undiminished, unless the firm ceases trading altogether.

4. W. O. Henderson, *Britain and Industrial Europe, 1750–1870* (Leicester, 1972); *106–33*.

5. It must be borne in mind that some large-scale business organisations continue to be dominated by individual owner-managers. However, they became an increasing anomaly amongst giant firms during the twentieth century, and their underlying fragility is suggested by the way in which Robert Maxwell's international business empire disintegrated following his sudden death in 1991.

6. W. Woodruff, *Impact of Western Man* (London, 1966); *254*.

7. L. Johnman, 'The Large Manufacturing Companies of 1935', *Business History*, XXVIII (1986); *239–41*. Unilever's world-wide workforce was just under 200,000.

8. Gross stock of domestic reproducible fixed assets; C. H. Feinstein and S. Pollard eds, *Studies in Capital Formation in the United Kingdom 1750–1920* (Oxford, 1988); *433–4*.

9. *Historical Statistics of the United States, Colonial Times to 1970* (Washington DC, 1975); II, *734*; T. R. Gourvish, *Railways and the British Economy 1830–1914* (London, 1980); *18*.

10. Payne's data were taken from the *Stock Exchange Year Book* for 1905, but refer to the previous year. Gross assets represent a balance-sheet assessment of the value of a firm's plant, materials, trade credits etc., while nominal, or authorised, capitalisation represents a (variable) legal limit on the sum which may be raised in share issues by a company. Nominal capital is, in turn, a less reliable measure of a firm's worth than the market valuation of issued capital (share price multiplied by number of shares outstanding); assuming that contemporary market wisdom is best placed to value a firm's current and future prospects. Further complication arises inasmuch as a firm's capitalisation, which invariably includes equity stock (conferring ' beneficial ownership, normally with no pre-determined level of dividend payments), may also include bonded, or debenture, stock (conferring no ownership and usually bearing fixed interest entitlement). The market capitalisation data presented in this study follow recent business practice in restricting coverage to equity stock. Consequently, some of these estimates differ from those in Hannah (1983; *102–3, 189–90*) and Chandler (1990; *666–79*), which appear to include debentures.

11. Table 1 excludes British-American Tobacco (BAT) with a market valuation of $158.9 million, established in 1902 with one-third British and two-thirds American ownership, but domiciled in Britain. Following a US Supreme Court ruling in 1911, the American stock holders were obliged to sell their stake in the enterprise, and by the 1920s BAT was wholly British owned. The rankings in Table 1 are derived, in part, from a more comprehensive listing of the world's hundred largest industrial firms of 1912/13, available in Schmitz, 1995.

12. The 25th ranking American and British industrials in 1937, for example, had market capitalisations of $335 million and $91 million respectively, while the equivalent German firm had gross assets of $52 million.

13. Table 2 does not imply any specific rankings for firms, given the differences between market capitalisation and assets highlighted in footnote 10. However it is certain that a majority of the world's top firms in the later 1930s in included, whatever measure is adopted. The precise definition of 'firms' would also affect rankings; if, for example, Royal Dutch-Shell was taken as a group, its capitalisation would have

amounted to $1983.4 million, making it the world's second biggest industrial organisation. The list excludes direct subsidiaries: for example the US-based Shell Union Corporation, with a market capitalisation of $357.8 million, which was wholly owned by the Royal Dutch-Shell group. Also excluded are a number of large US firms which were predominantly involved in retailing: F W Woolworth (capitalisation $482.1 million), Sears Roebuck ($410.0 million), Montgomery Ward ($286.2 million), J C Penny ($205.1 million) and Great Atlantic & Pacific Tea ($201.7 million). The general question of whether service sector firms should be included in such listings is discussed, amongst other places, in Wardley, 1991 and Schmitz, 1995.

14. National product estimates (GNP USA and UK, NNP France and Germany) are derived from data in B. R. Mitchell, *European Historical Statistics, 1750–1975* (London, 1981); *821, 826* and B. R. Mitchell, *International Historical Statistics: the Americas and Australasia* (London, 1983); *889, 897*. The market valuation of American and British firms and the gross assets of German firms are taken from the data sets summarised in Tables 1 and 2; the market valuation of the top 25 French firms is given by Lévy-Leboyer (in Chandler and Daems, 1980; *130*).

15. Between 1897 and 1940, Canada and Latin America consistently received 70 to 75 per cent of American FDI (Wilkins, 1970; *110*; 1974; *55, 182–3*), while in the period 1900 to 1939, between 70 and 88 per cent of continental European multinational subsidiaries were located within Europe (Franko, 1976; *92*). In contrast, a sample of British manufacturing multinationals of the period 1870–1939 reveals a wide dispersal of subsidiaries; including 26 per cent in the Americas, 23 per cent in Europe, 22 per cent in Australasia and 13 per cent in South Africa; S. J. Nicholas, 'British Multinational Investment before 1939' *Journal of European Economic History*, XI (1982); *625*.

16. *An Inquiry into the Nature and Causes of the Wealth of Nations*, (ed. E. Cannan, London, 1904; 6th edn 1950); I, *144*.

17. A natural monopoly occurs when technical factors dictate that optimal efficiency is achieved by a single operator in an industry. With utilities like water or gas supply the vast majority of costs are 'overheads', representing huge fixed investment in plant and distribution networks. The futility of duplicating such systems was demonstrated early in the nineteenth century; instead governments increasingly tolerated such monopolies, subject to statutory regulation (Hannah, in Nakagawa, 1980; *108–11*).

18. A. Gerschenkron, *Economic Backwardness in Historical Perspective* (Cambridge MA, 1962) argues that when 'latecomers' to economic development desire to achieve rapid industrialisation (the classic

example being Tsarist Russia), state intervention and bank capital may be employed to compensate for deficiencies in private-sector entrepreneurial skills and capital accumulation.

19. For a critique of Marglin's thesis, see: D. S. Landes, 'What do Bosses Really Do?' *Journal of Economic History*, XLVI (1986); *585–623*.

20. Key aspects of Lenin's analysis, linking the growth of big business with imperialism, are convincingly undermined, amongst other places, in: D. K. Fieldhouse, *Economics and Empire, 1830–1914* (London, 1973); *38–53*.

21. *Statistical Abstract of the United States, 1906* (Washington DC, 1907); *40*; H. Perkin, *The Rise of Professional Society: England since 1880* (London, 1989); *80*; M. G. Mulhall, *Dictionary of Statistics* (London, 1909); *354*.

22. Derived from data in: A. Maddison, *Phases of Capitalist Development* (Oxford, 1982); *161, 180–3*.

23. *Historical Statistics of the United States*; II, *716*; Mitchell, *European Historical Statistics, 1750–1975*; *668, 670*.

24. E. I. Du Pont de Nemours & Co., *Du Pont: The Autobiography of an American Enterprise* (Wilmington DE, 1952); *21, 131*.

25. *Historical Statistics of the United States*; II, *783–4*; *Statistical Abstract for the United Kingdom, 1908–1922* (London, 1924); *307*.

26. *The Age of Reform: From Bryan to F. D. R.* (New York, 1955); *23–59*.

27. The classic statement of this thesis is: R. H. Wiebe, *The Search for Order, 1877–1920* (New York, 1967).

28. Average annual compound growth rates of per capita GDP at constant prices; Maddison, *Phases of Capitalist Development*; *44*.

Select bibliography

Despite John Kenneth Galbraith declaring that 'few subjects of solemn inquiry have been more unproductive than study of the modern large corporation' (1972; *87*), recent years have witnessed phenomenal growth in the literature relating to the theory of the firm, the rise of managerial capitalism and the multinational corporation, as well as empirical company histories and industry studies. Consequently, this bibliography is highly selective. It is also largely restricted to works in English.

A wider range of key research papers in this subject area are conveniently brought together in a new series, 'The International Library of Critical Writings in Business History', edited by Geoffrey Jones and published by Edward Elgar. Of particular relevance is volume five in the series: *The Rise of Big Business* (1992), edited by Barry Supple, and containing 23 seminal articles originally published between 1932 and 1991.

Invaluable guides to the major theoretical contributions in this area are provided by Caves (1982) and Clarke and McGuinness (1987). An extensive body of American and British business history is accessible through two comprehensive listings: *Corporate America: A Historical Bibliography* (New York: ABC-Clio, 1984) and F. Goodall, *A Bibliography of British Business Histories* (London: Gower, 1987). These are particularly useful for locating individual company histories, only a few major examples of which are listed here. On a broader front, an authoritative reference work containing brief historical sketches of some 1,250 of the world's largest firms of the 1980s, arranged in industry groups, is: T. Derdak and L. Mirabik (eds), *International Directory of Company Histories*, 6 vols (London: St. James Press, 1988–94). Concise biographies of British and American business leaders are available in: D. J. Jeremy and C. Shaw (eds), *Dictionary of Business Biography*, 5 vols (London: Butterworth, 1984–6), A. Slaven and S. G. Checkland (eds), *Dictionary of Scottish Business Biography, 1860–1960*, 2 vols (Aberdeen, 1986, 90) and J. Ingham, *Biographical Dictionary of American Business Leaders*, 4 vols (Westport CT: Greenwood, 1983).

Alford, B. W. E. (1973) *W D & H O Wills and the Development of the UK Tobacco Industry 1786–1965* (London: Methuen); valuable case-study of a leading family-dominated enterprise.

Atack, J. (1986) 'Firm Size and Industrial Structure in the United States during the Nineteenth Century', *Journal of Economic History*, XLVI; qualifies aspects of the Chandler (1977) thesis by arguing that transportation developments before 1870 had a mixed impact on industrial concentration, with the proportion of small firms increasing markedly in many areas of manufacturing.

Baran, P. and Sweezy, P. M. (1966) *Monopoly Capital: An Essay on the American Economic and Social Order* (New York: Monthly Review Press); classic Marxist viewpoint on the rise of the corporate economy, although it concentrates rather more on the consequences than the origins of corporate capitalism.

Berle, A. A. and Mearns, C. G. (1932) *The Modern Corporation and Private Property* (New York: Macmillan); seminal study which drew attention to the growing divorce of ownership and control in leading American corporations.

Born, K. E. (1983) *International Banking in the 19th and 20th Centuries* (Leamington Spa: Berg); detailed account of the development of world banking and its relations with industry since the early nineteenth century.

Braverman, H. (1974) *Labor and Monopoly Capital* (New York: Monthly Review Press); stimulating Marxist analysis of the impact of mass production techniques on the labour force, particularly useful for its discussion of the dangers of worker alienation within the large corporation.

Cain, P. J. (1972) 'Railway Combination and Government 1900–14', *Economic History Review*, 2nd Series, XXV; surveys the ambiguous attitude of British government towards attempts by railway companies to amalgamate, in order to achieve efficiency of operation.

Cairncross, A. K. and Hunter, J. B. K. (1987) 'The Early Growth of Messrs. J. & P. Coats, 1830–1883', *Business History*, XXIX; valuable reminder of the potential for internal expansion within a company – charting how the early growth of one of Britain's largest manufacturing firms occurred mainly on the basis of reinvested profits.

Caron, F. (1973) *Histoire de l'Exploitation d'un Grand Réseau: La Compagnie du Chemin de Fer du Nord, 1846–1937* (Paris: Mouton); detailed study of France's largest railway company, which tends to concentrate more on the growth of traffic and factors affecting profitability, rather than the development of managerial organisation.

Carosso, V. P. (1970) *Investment Banking in America* (Cambridge MA:

Harvard); surveys the growth of investment banking from the early railroad era until the Second World War, as well as the regulatory legislation affecting it.

Carosso, V. P. (1987) *The Morgans: Private International Bankers, 1854–1913* (Cambridge MA: Harvard); definitive study of the leading American investment banking house of the late nineteenth and early twentieth century.

Carter, E. C., Foster, R. and Moody, J. N. (eds) (1976) *Enterprise and Entrepreneurs in Nineteenth and Twentieth Century France* (Baltimore: Johns Hopkins); useful collection, including contributions by Charles Kindleberger, Maurice Lévy-Leboyer and David Landes, which goes some way towards correcting a conventional unduly pessimistic view of French entrepreneurship and industrial structure.

Caves, R. E. (1982) *Multinational Enterprise and Economic Analysis* (Cambridge); comprehensive and critical survey of the literature.

Chandler, A. D. Jr. (1962) *Strategy and Structure: Chapters in the History of American Industrial Enterprise* (Cambridge MA: MIT); the first major statement by Chandler of his thesis concerning the growth of American business enterprise, in particular the M-form structures of the post 1920 era; establishing the case for an approach in terms of technology, markets and managerial hierarchies.

Chandler, A. D. Jr. (1965) 'The Railroads: Pioneers in Modern Corporate Management', *Business History Review*, XXXIX; stresses the significance of railroads as the testing grounds for new forms of managerial organisation and industrial finance.

Chandler, A. D. Jr. (1969) 'The Structure of American Industry in the Twentieth Century: A Historical Overview', *Business History Review*, XLIII; provides valuable data (compiled by G. Porter and H. Livesay) on oligopoly control and the growth of diversification in leading US industrials between 1909 and 1960.

Chandler, A. D. Jr. (1977) *The Visible Hand: The Managerial Revolution in American Business* (Cambridge MA: Harvard); a major elaboration on his earlier work, tracing the rise of managerial capitalism in the United States between the 1840s and the 1920s. In terms of its world-wide impact, this has probably been the most influential single contribution to the historical study of corporate growth to appear to date.

Chandler, A. D. Jr. (1990) *Scope and Scale: The Dynamics of Industrial Capitalism* (Cambridge MA: Harvard); magisterial comparison of the development of managerial capitalism in the United States with the experience of Britain and Germany, which will undoubtedly set the agenda for much future research in business history.

Chandler, A. D. Jr. and Daems, H. (eds) (1980) *Managerial Hierarchies:*

Comparative Perspectives on the Rise of the Modern Industrial Enterprise
(Cambridge MA: Harvard); an important collection of papers
which elaborate on themes raised by Chandler (1977) – of particular value in assessing the applicability of the 'visible hand'
concept of managerial capitalism in Britain, Germany and France,
as well as a more general critique of this thesis by Oliver Williamson.

Chapman, S. D. (1985) 'British-based Investment Groups before 1914'
Economic History Review, 2nd Series, XXXVIII; implies that the
apparent fragmented, small-scale nature of British enterprise in the
field of foreign direct investment, masks more extensive, informal
networks of business interest.

Chaudhuri, K. N. (1978) *The Trading World of Asia and the English East
India Company, 1660–1760* (Cambridge); a valuable reminder that,
in certain high-risk contexts, large-scale business enterprise and
complex forms of managerial organisation were not uniquely
products of the nineteenth and twentieth centuries.

Clarke, R. and McGuinness, T. (eds) (1987) *The Economics of the Firm*
(Oxford: Blackwell); very accessible survey of key aspects of the
theory of the firm, including chapters on vertical integration,
managerial hierarchies and multinational enterprise.

Coase, R. H. (1937) 'The Nature of the Firm', *Economica*, IV; seminal
article which laid the groundwork for the transaction costs
approach to corporate growth, in particular as elaborated by
Williamson (1975, 1985, 1986).

Coleman, D. C. (1969) *Courtaulds: An Economic and Social History*, 2 vols
(Oxford); detailed study of a highly successful family-controlled
British textile firm, which expanded very rapidly in the early
twentieth century.

Coleman, D. C. (1987) 'The Uses and Abuses of Business History',
Business History, XXXIX; valuable review of achievements and
shortcomings in recent business history, pinpointing difficulties in
applying aspects of theory (for example, transaction costs) to the
historical record.

Collins, M. (1991) *Banks and Industrial Finance in Britain 1800–1939*
(London: Macmillan); very concise survey of the relationships
between the financial sector and British business, concluding that
far more historical evidence is required before any definitive judge-
ments can be formed.

Davis, L. E. (1966) 'Capital Markets and Industrial Concentration: The
U.S. and U.K., a Comparative Study', *Economic History Review*,
2nd Series, XIX; argues that differences in concentration levels in
UK and US industry can be explained to a large extent in terms of
their respective access to stock market funds.

Dunning, J. H. (1988) *Explaining International Production* (London: Unwin Hyman); particularly valuable for the author's attempt at an 'eclectic' theory of multinational enterprise, as well as some useful historical perspectives on the growth of international business.

Eichner, A. S. (1969) *The Emergence of Oligopoly: Sugar Refining as a Case Study* (Baltimore: Johns Hopkins); an important American case study which stresses that mergers in the sugar industry were motivated more by a desire to control prices than to achieve economies of scale.

Eis, C. (1969) 'The 1919–1930 Merger Movement in American Industry', *Journal of Law and Economics*, XII; presents an alternative set of merger data to set alongside that provided by Nelson (1959).

Elbaum, B. and Lazonick, W. (eds) (1986) *The Decline of the British Economy* (Oxford); important set of papers which jointly make a case for relative UK retardation arising from a series of institutional rigidities, amongst which were weak industry-capital market links and an adherence to small-scale business organisation, unlike the USA, where large-scale firms reaped benefits from the visible hand of managerial coordination.

Farnie, D. and Yonekawa, S. (1988) 'The Emergence of the Large Firm in the Cotton Spinning Industries of the World, 1883–1938', *Textile History*, XIX; detailed survey which contrasts a general lack of vertical integration amongst UK cotton spinners compared with elsewhere, as well as illustrating a general decline in family-centred firms.

Feldenkirchen, W. (1987) 'Big Business in Interwar Germany: Organizational Innovation at Vereinigte Stahlwerke, IG Farben and Siemens' *Business History Review*, LXI; examines the role of interwar economic dislocation in promoting rationalisation and concentration.

Ferrier, R. W. (1982) *The History of the British Petroleum Company, I: The Developing Years, 1901–1932* (Cambridge); weighty account of the emergence of a leading British multinational, placing considerable emphasis on organisational innovation.

Field, A. J. (1987) 'Modern Business Enterprise as a Capital-Saving Innovation', *Journal of Economic History*, LXVII; unlike Habakkuk (1962), argues that the net effect of technological and organisational innovation was not labour saving, but to spread the costs of holding capital over larger volumes of output.

Franko, L. G. (1976) *The European Multinationals: A Renewed Challenge to American and British Business* (New York: Harper & Row); surveys the evolution of continental European multinationals since the late nineteenth century.

Fridenson, P. (1972) *L'histoire des Usines Renault: I, Naissance de la grande enterprise 1898–1939* (Paris: Seuil); study of a leading French automobile manufacturer which was dominated by its founder-owner.

Galambos, L. (1975) *The Public Image of Big Business in America 1880–1940: A Quantitative Study in Social Change* (Baltimore: Johns Hopkins); examines popular perceptions of big business through a complex analysis of press coverage of corporate affairs.

Galbraith, J. K. (1972) *The New Industrial State* (London: Andre Deutsch, 2nd edn); characteristically provocative thesis, suggesting the historical evolution of a big business-government 'technostructure'.

Gourvish, T. R. (1973) 'A British Business Elite: The Chief Executive Managers of the Railway Industry, 1850–1923', *Business History Review*, XLVII; demonstrates that innovations in business structures and managerial practices in British railway firms mirrored those in American railroads.

Habakkuk, H. J. (1962) *American and British Technology in the Nineteenth Century* (Cambridge); provides valuable perspectives on factor-biased technological changes in business, in particular adoption of labour-saving devices by US firms to economise in a situation of relatively high wages.

Hannah, L. (ed) (1982) *From Family Firm in Professional Management: Structure and Performance of Business Enterprise* (Budapest: 8th International Economic History Congress); collection of papers stressing the continuing importance of family enterprise in many areas of European big business until the 1950s.

Hannah, L. (1983) *The Rise of the Corporate Economy* (London: Methuen, 2nd edn); standard account of the development of managerial capitalism in Britain, which stresses the importance of merger activity in the increasing concentration of British manufacturing industry since the late nineteenth century, unlike Prais (1976).

Harvey, C. E. (1981) *The Rio Tinto Company: An Economic History of the Leading International Mining Concern, 1873–1954* (Penzance: Hodge); case study of one of Britain's leading international firms, in a sector not often considered in discussion of the modern business enterprise.

Hawley, E. W. (1966) *The New Deal and the Problem of Monopoly: A Study in Ambivalence* (Princeton); suggests that federal agencies encountered difficulties in reconciling anti-trust sentiment with a desire for national economic recovery during the 1930s.

Hayes, P. (1987) *Industry and Ideology: IG Farben in the Nazi Era* (Cambridge); detailed study of Germany's largest industrial corporation of the interwar period, which throws particular light on the firm's relationship with the state.

Hertner, P. and Jones, G. (eds) (1986) *Multinationals: Theory and History* (London: Gower); a useful review of theoretical approaches, plus case studies of French, German and Swedish multinationals.

Hidy, R. W. and Hidy, M. E. (1955) *Pioneering in Big Business, 1882–1911: History of Standard Oil (New Jersey)* (New York: Harper); an influential study of the development of the world's largest enterprise in the pre-1914 petroleum industry.

Hilferding, R. (1910) *Finance Capital: A Study of the Latest Phase of Capitalist Development* (new edn T. Bottomore, London: Routledge & Kegan Paul, 1981); stresses the role of bank interests in promoting large-scale business enterprise, and influential in the formulation of later Marxist theory, including that of Lenin (1917).

Horn, N. and Kocka, J. (eds) (1979) *Recht und Entwicklung der Grossunternehmen in 19. und frühen 20. Jahrhundert – Law and the Formation of the Big Enterprises in the 19th and Early 20th Centuries* (Göttingen: Vandenhoeck & Ruprecht); an important collection of papers examining the influence of socio-legal factors in the relative growth of European and American big business.

Hounshell, D. A. (1984) *From the American System to Mass Production, 1800–1932: The development of Manufacturing Technology in the United States* (Baltimore: Johns Hopkins); a comprehensive survey of the evolution of American mass production techniques, particularly valuable for its discussion of Henry Ford's innovations in manufacturing organisation.

Hounshell, D. A. and Smith, J. K. (1988) *Science and Corporate Strategy: Du Pont R & D 1902–1980* (Cambridge); definitive study of the corporate research effort in one of America's most innovative manufacturers.

Houssiaux, J. (1958) *Le Pouvoir de Monopole* (Paris: Sirey); dated, but still useful for its discussion of business concentration and merger activity in the twentieth century French economy.

Irving, R. J. (1976) *The North Eastern Railway Company 1870–1914* (Leicester); one of the few studies of management and business organisation in the British railway sector.

Jones, G. (ed.) (1986) *British Multinationals: Origins, Management and Performance* (London: Gower); concise historical studies of British multinationals, including Dunlop, Cadbury, Glaxo and Pilkington.

Jones, R. and Marriott, O. (1970) *Anatomy of a Merger: A History of G.E.C., A.E.I. and English Electric* (London: Jonathan Cape); rather sketchy but informative survey of corporate growth, cartels and mergers in the electric industry since the 1880s.

Kennedy, W. P. (1987) *Industrial Structure, Capital Markets and the Origins of British Economic Decline* (Cambridge); argues that pre-1914 Britain failed to develop large-scale industries in new technologies like chemicals and electricals, due to a basic failing in the capital market, which preferred to channel British funds into foreign investments.

Kobayashi, K. and Morikawa, H. (eds) (1986) *Development of Managerial Enterprise* (Fuji International Conferences on Business History, 12; Tokyo); one of a valuable series of Japanese-sponsored conference papers, contrasting the development of managerial enterprises in America, Europe and Asia.

Kocka, J. (1971) 'Family and Bureaucracy in German Industrial Management 1850–1914: Siemens in Comparative Perspective' *Business History Review*, XLV; argues that Siemens developed aspects of a multi-divisional structure before World War I, ahead of its more widely known adoption in the USA.

Kolko, G. (1963) *The Triumph of Conservatism: A Reinterpretation of American History, 1900–1916* (New York: Free Press); a controversial neo-Marxist interpretation which suggests that federal antitrust legislation, as well as wider aspects of the progressive response to big business, were influenced by the business community to their own ends.

Kolko, G. (1965) *Railroads and Regulation 1877–1916* (Princeton); extends his (1963) analysis to the railroad industry, which he also suggests benefitted from federal regulation. This view should be contrasted with the thesis proposed by Martin (1971).

Lamoreaux, N. (1985) *The Great Merger Movement in American Business, 1895–1904* (Cambridge); a valuable analysis of an important period of merger activity in the USA, which suggests the movement only had a limited effect on reducing competitive forces in the market.

Landes, D. S. (1949) 'French Entrepreneurship and Industrial Growth in the Nineteenth Century', *Journal of Economic History*, IX; classic statement of the view that French entrepreneurship failed to provide a vital source of growth for the economy, being particularly dominated by conservative family-centred firms. However, this thesis has been contested in more recent scholarship – see, for example, Nye (1987) – and Landes himself has qualified his earlier harsh judgement in Carter, Foster and Moody (eds) (1976).

Landes, D. S. (1969) *The Unbound Prometheus: Technological Change and Industrial Development in Western Europe from 1750 to the Present* (Cambridge); a major study of European industrialisation which, amongst other things, emphasises the relative small-scale and technological retardation of British and French business enterprise from the later nineteenth century, compared with that in Germany and the USA.

Langlois, R. N. and Robertson, P. L. (1989) 'Explaining Vertical Integration: Lessons from the American Automobile Industry', *Journal of Economic History*, XLIX; find that a transaction costs approach provides the most convincing explanation of integration in the car industry.

Laux, J. M. (1976) *In First Gear: The French Automobile Industry to 1914* (Liverpool); an accessible account of this untypically dynamic sector of French industry.

Lee, C. H. (1990) 'Corporate Behaviour in Theory and History: I. The Evolution of Theory'; 'II. The Historian's Perspective', *Business History*, XXXII; concise surveys of the major theoretical and empirical approaches to the rise of the modern business corporation.

Lenin, V. I. (1917) *Imperialism: The Highest Stage of Capitalism* (Moscow: Progress Publishers, 1978 edn); the classic view of a world of monopoly capitalism transmuting into a state of global imperialism; despite its shortcomings, a major influence on almost all subsequent Marxist work on big business and imperialism.

McCraw, T. K. (1984) *Prophets of Regulation* (Cambridge MA: Harvard); an important survey of leading American protagonists in government-business relations, including Charles F. Adams and Louis D. Brandeis, as well as wider aspects of the regulatory framework.

Macrosty, H. W. (1907) *The Trust Movement in British Industry* (London: Longman); detailed and generally critical account of cartels and mergers in Britain.

Marglin, S. (1974) 'What Do Bosses Do? The Origins and Functions of Hierarchy in Capitalist Production', *Review of Radical Political Economy*, VI; a much-cited Marxist interpretation of the large-scale firm as an instrument to control the work environment and wages of the labour force.

Martin, A. (1971) *Enterprise Denied: Origins of the Decline of American Railroads 1897–1917* (New York: Columbia); suggests the heavy hand of government regulation was a major factor in the long-run decline of US railroads – an argument to be contrasted with the position adopted by Kolko (1965).

Maschke, E. (1969) 'Outline of the History of German Cartels from 1873 to 1914' in F. Crouzet, W. H. Chaloner and W. Stern (eds), *Essays in European Economic History, 1789–1914* (London: Arnold); heavy-going but valuable survey of the massive cartelisation of pre-1914 German industry.

Michie, R. (1988) 'Different in name only?: The London Stock Exchange and Foreign Bourses, c. 1850–1914', *Business History*, XXX; suggests that large-scale business organisation in Germany was, in part, a response to greater difficulties in raising capital from equity markets, compared with the situation in Britain.

Mowery, D. C. (1983) 'Industrial Research and Firm Size, Survival and

Growth in American Manufacturing 1921–1946: an Assessment', *Journal of Economic History*, XLIII; finds a weak correlation between corporate size and research commitment in US industry.

Mueller, D. C. (1986) *The Modern Corporation: Profits, Power, Growth and Performance* (Brighton: Wheatsheaf); a collection of the author's major journal articles on corporate structure and growth.

Nakagawa, K. (ed.) (1977) *Social Order and Entrepreneurship* (Fuji International Conferences on Business History, 2; Tokyo); conference papers dealing with socio-economic influences on comparative business organisation in the USA, Europe and Asia.

Nakagawa, K. (ed) (1980) *Government and Business* (Fuji International Conferences on Business History, 5; Tokyo); collected papers on government-business relations in Europe, America and Japan.

Navin, T. R. and Sears, M. V. (1955) 'The Rise of a Market for Industrial Securities, 1887–1902', *Business History Review*, XXXIX; valuable article charting the evolution of American stock markets and their influence on industrial finance.

Nelson, R. L. (1959) *Merger Movements in American Industry, 1895–1956* (Princeton: National Bureau of Economic and Social Research); still the major statistical source for US merger activity, although superseded in part by the work of Eis (1969).

Neuburger, H. (1977) 'The Industrial Policies of the Kreditbanken, 1880–1914', *Business History Review*, LI; despite suggesting that bank finance actively promoted industrial consolidations, finds little evidence to support Hilferding's view that financial interests dominated industrial management.

Neuburger, H. and Stokes, H. H. (1974) 'German Banks and German Growth, 1883–1913: An Empirical View', *Journal of Economic History*, XXXIV; argue that bank finance was biased towards heavy industry and large-scale consolidations, thus promoting these sectors in the German economy at the expense of light, consumer goods industries, as well as furthering business concentration.

Nevins, A. (1940) *John D. Rockefeller: The Heroic Age of American Enterprise*, 2 vols. (New York: Scribner's); authorised biography of the world's wealthiest industrialist of his era, which tends towards a rather sympathetic viewpoint, unlike Tarbell (1904).

Nevins, A. and Hill, F. E. (1954, 57, 63) *Ford*, 3 vols (New York: Scribner's); an accomplished but generally sympathetic portrait of America's second largest automobile corporation and its founder.

Nye, J. V. (1987) 'Firm Size and Economic Backwardness: A New Look at the French Industrialization Debate', *Journal of Economic History*, XLVII; argues that small firms were not a significant impediment to French economic performance, and were a function of prevailing economic and technological conditions.

O'Brien, A. P. (1988) 'Factory Size, Economies of Scale and the Great Merger Wave of 1898–1902', *Journal of Economic History*, XLVIII; argues that US factory sizes grew more rapidly during the 1869–89 period than 1899–1929, suggesting that economies of scale were not an important motive in the great merger wave.

Okochi, A. and Yasuoka, S. (eds) (1984) *Family Business in the Era of Industrial Growth* (Fuji International Conferences on Business History, 10; Tokyo); mixed collection of papers; particularly valuable for contributions on family-centred enterprise in Britain, France, Germany and the United States.

Payne, P. L. (1967) 'The Emergence of the Large-scale Company in Great Britain, 1870–1914', *Economic History Review*, 2nd Ser., XX; presents a widely-cited ranking of leading UK industrial firms around 1904–05, as well as a critical survey of factors inhibiting the growth of large-scale enterprise.

Payne, P. L. (1988) *British Entrepreneurship in the Nineteenth Century* (London: Macmillan, 2nd edn); a concise review of business organisation and entrepreneurial performance during an era of relative economic decline.

Penrose, E. T. (1959) *The Theory of the Growth of the Firm* (Oxford: Blackwell); an influential contribution to the theory of corporate growth, with particular emphasis on economies of scope achieved through product diversification.

Pohl, H. (ed.) (1988) *The Concentration Process in the Entrepreneurial Economy since the late 19th Century* (Stuttgart, *Zeitschrift für Unternehmensgeschichte* 55); studies of rather mixed quality, examining aspects of business concentration in France, Germany, Sweden and the United States.

Pollard, S. (1965) *The Genesis of Modern Management* (London, Arnold); a stimulating survey of managerial organisation in Britain up to the mid nineteenth century.

Prais, S. J. (1976) *The Evolution of Giant Firms in Britain* (Cambridge); a careful analysis of the growth of large firms in British industry between 1909 and 1970, which argues that internal growth was responsible for a larger part of increasing concentration, in contrast to Hannah (1983).

Reader, W. J. (1970, 75) *Imperial Chemical Industries: a history*, 2 vols (Oxford); major study of Britain's leading chemicals firm.

Rubinstein, W. D. (1993) *Capitalism, Culture and Decline in Britain, 1750–1990* (London: Routledge); a vigorous attack upon traditionally formulated accounts of Britain's relative economic decline, and upon the view, expressed in particular by Wiener (1981), that a pervasive anti-industrial culture inhibited British managerial innovation and economic growth.

Schmitz, C. J. (1986) 'The Rise of Big Business in the World Copper Industry, 1870–1930', *Economic History Review*, 2nd Ser., XXXIX; stresses the role of technological factors, rather than transaction costs, in promoting concentration in the mining and smelting sector.

Schmitz, C. J. (1995) 'The World's Largest Industrial Companies of 1912', *Business History*, XXXVII; provides listings of a hundred leading firms, and lends support to the view expressed recently, amongst others by Wardley (1991), that the largest US firms were not of a greatly dissimilar order of magnitude to their British or German counterparts in the pre-First World War era.

Scott, J. D. (1962) *Vickers: A History* (London: Weidenfeld and Nicolson); informative study of a major British armaments, shipbuilding and engineering firm.

Scott, J. P. (1985) *Corporations, Classes and Capitalism* (London: Hutchinson, 2nd edn); a useful, if at times rather convoluted survey of American and European corporate enterprise, largely from the perspective of sociological theory.

Scott, J. P. and Griff, C. (1984) *Directors of Industry: The British Corporate Network, 1904–76* (Cambridge: Polity Press); rather inconclusively argues for the importance of informal networks of control in British business, as represented by interlocking directorships.

Semmler, W. (1982) 'Theories of Competition and Monopoly', *Capital and Class*, 18; a neo-Marxist critique of theories of monopoly capitalism.

Siemens, G. (1957) *History of the house of Siemens*, 2 vols (Freiburg-Munich: Karl Alber); lengthy and rather dull history of the leading German electrical firm.

Sklar, M. J. (1988) *The Corporate Reconstruction of American Capitalism 1890–1916: The Market, the Law and Politics* (Cambridge); examines the complex interplay between economic and social theory, law and the business community in a period of increasing debate about the regulation of big business.

Sloan, A. P. (1963) *My Years with General Motors* (New York: Doubleday); an inside view of corporate strategy by the leading executive in one of the world's largest industrial firms of the post World War I era.

Tarbell, I. M. (1904) *The History of the Standard Oil Company* (New York: Macmillan); firmly in the 'muckraking' tradition, a spirited attack by the daughter of an oilman ruined by Standard Oil's founder, John D. Rockefeller.

Tilly, R. (1982) 'Mergers, External Growth and Finance in the Development of Large-Scale Enterprise in Germany 1880–1913, *Journal of Economic History*, XLII; suggests that whilst external growth was frequently crucial for the expansion of individual concerns, mergers accounted for no more than one-fifth of overall corporate growth.

Turner, H. A. (1985) *German Big Business and the Rise of Hitler* (Oxford); argues, unlike Marxist historiography, that German big business did not systematically support Hitler's rise to power and that the Nazis had a confused and inconsistent policy towards large-scale capitalism.

Wall, J. (1970) *Andrew Carnegie* (Oxford); definitive biography of American's leading steel manufacturer in the last quarter of the nineteenth century.

Wardley, P. (1991) 'The Anatomy of Big Business: Aspects of Corporate Development in the Twentieth Century', *Business History*, XXXIII; a survey of Britain's largest enterprises between about 1904 and 1985, which is particularly valuable for underlining the continuing predominance of firms in the service sector.

Webb, S. B. (1980) 'Tariffs, Cartels, Technology and Growth in the German Steel Industry 1879–1914', *Journal of Economic History*, XL; finds that cartels and tariffs, in conjunction, systematically favoured larger steel firms, which were then able to grow at the expense of smaller producers.

Wiener, M. J. (1981) *English Culture and the Decline of the Industrial Spirit, 1850–1980* (Cambridge); controversial expression of the view that British industrial decline was largely determined by a profound anti-business culture evident in the nation's commercial, financial and political elites – a view contested, most prominently, by Rubinstein (1993).

Wilkins, M. (1970) *The Emergence of Multinational Enterprise: American Business Abroad from the Colonial era to 1914* (Cambridge MA: Harvard); definitive account of early American multinationals.

Wilkins, M. (1974) *The Maturing of Multinational Enterprise: American Business Abroad from 1914 to 1970* (Cambridge MA: Harvard); authoritative and detailed continuation of this major study of American multinationals.

Wilkins, M. (1988) 'European and North American Multinationals 1870–1914: Comparisons and Contrasts', *Business History*, XXX; wide-ranging surveys which finds, amongst other things, that banks were more instrumental in promoting German and Swedish based MNE than that from other nations, and that British MNE particularly excelled in consumer goods.

Williamson, O. E. (1975) *Markets and Hierarchies: Analysis and Antitrust Implications* (New York: Free Press); influential theoretical study which stresses transaction cost motives in corporate growth, very much inspired by the pioneering work of Coase (1937).

Williamson, O. E. (1985) *The Economic Institutions of Capitalism: Firms,*

Markets, Relational Contracting (New York: Free Press); elaboration of the author's earlier work, with more appreciation of historical perspectives.

Williamson, O. E. (1986) *Economic Organization: Firms, Markets and Policy Control* (Brighton: Wheatsheaf); a collection of the author's major journal articles.

Wilson, C. (1954) *The History of Unilever: A Study of Economic Growth and Social Change*, 2 vols (London: Cassel); a pioneering British business history, examining the growth of a leading Anglo-Dutch multinational.

Index

New Studies in Economic and Social History

Previously published as

Studies in Economic History

Titles in the series available from the Macmillan Press Limited

Economic History Society

The Economic History Society, which numbers around 3,000 members, publishes the *Economic History Review* four times a year (free to members) and holds an annual conference.

Enquiries about membership should be addressed to

The Assistant Secretary
Economic History Society
PO Box 70
Kingswood
Bristol
BS15 5TB

Full-time students may join at special rates.